Judaism and the Community

Judaism and the Community:

New Directions in Jewish Social Work

Edited by Dr. Jacob Freid,
Executive Director, Jewish Braille Institute of America

South Brunswick
New York ● Thomas Yoseloff ● London

Introduction

In 1933, exactly one third of a century ago, Franklin Delano Roosevelt and Adolf Hitler assumed the chief executive power of their respective nations at a time when a national economic and political crisis was sweeping across the United States and Germany. The opposite use each made of his power as the ultimate "yes" of a polity and people *in extremis* is still serving historians, political scientists, and social psychologists as a classical demonstration of the different methods and ends of democracy and totalitarianism in a period of acute national distress. To the Jews, the stark contrast was, and is, more than academic. It is imbued with life and death, with the mute testimony of six million witnesses in Germany, where almost all the self-contained Jewish communities today are cemeteries. In the United States, existence for the Jews has been that of a completely different kind — a flourishing *Etz Chaim,* so that today American Jewry has achieved a status of prosperity — synagogue affiliation and religious school attendance are unmatched in Jewish history, particularly in the greatest single center of Jewish life today, New York, which is served by the Federation of Jewish Philanthropies of New York.

5

The third of the century since 1933 has been a period of double climacteric for the Jewish people. The horror of Hitler and the miracle of Israel redeemed were still, in that order, but a dread and a hope in 1933. Today *shtetl* life is a wraith of memory, nostalgically recreated by Chagall's paintings, the musical "Fiddler on The Roof" and the reprints of Sholom Aleichem's stories.

Today New York City is a focal center of both Diaspora and American Jewish life. Bound up in the positive and negative aspects of its communal life are significant answers to what has happened to Jews and Jewish life in the principal Jewish communities in the United States, of which New York is first and foremost.

Here, in metropolitan New York, an area served by the largest professional complex of communal social, health, and welfare agencies in Jewish life anywhere in the world, are outlined in bold relief the significant trends in Jewish existence in this generation and the next. Here is highlighted the question of whether creative Jewish living is possible in the Diaspora, particularly in America, which has become the first magnitude new gravitational center of world Jewry in the wake of the destruction of the East European hub of Jewish culture, scholarship, and religion.

The American Jewish community, even more than the general public, has been subjected to the severe strains of a post-World-War-II reaction to the suburbs, automation, East–West conflict in a time of thermo-nuclear weapons, the existentialist philosophy of negativism, the precocious rush of adolescence to usurp the symbols of maturity (smoking, drinking, drugs, "hell-raising" for kicks, etc.). In addition, our Jewish community has had to resist the pull of assimilation. The result has been increasing acculturation and accommodation to American society. The problem has been how to permit the proper expression of the former without doing violence to the Jewish cultural and spiritual heritage and family and community pattern of life. The extent to which this struggle is succeeding is seen in the tremendous increase in attendance in our religious schools and synagogue affiliations. The extent to which it is failing is seen in the increased incidence of symptoms of malaise, virtually unknown in Jewish life in past generations in such degree and number. We refer to the alarming increase in the incidence of divorce, alcoholism, delinquency, the increasing incidence of inter-marriage, psychoneuroses, the weakening of the influence of the father in the home, etc.

During the present transitional stage of urban and suburban Jewish life, the Federation of Jewish Philanthropies contains the foremost peripatetic university of social welfare, health, and communal expertise in the United States of America, and, indeed, the world. This is a contemporary storehouse of knowledge, information, insight, and guidance into the crucial problems and anxieties and pressures of contemporary urban life waiting to be tapped by the Jewish community for its guidance and benefit. Their professional knowledge and experience gives guidance to our Greater New York Jewish community and to all Jewish metropolitan communities upon those matters which so profoundly concern us in our world today.

The essays which follow are concerned with Judaism and its present-day relationship to the community, social welfare, intermarriage, philanthropy, and mental health. The volume which preceded this surveyed the new ground broken by the Commission on Synagogue Relations between the rabbi and the social worker, in pioneering cooperation and understanding between them in the service of the community. The present volume points to "New Directions in Jewish Social Work." Its authors grapple with the raison d'être of the Jewish social agency in a predominantly non-Jewish culture. The rabbis are neither Pollyannas nor Cassandras—or should we say Jeremiahs. Nor are they Jonahs. They do not flinch from going to Nineveh, nor do they overlook the serious problems that confront Jewish life today.

The understanding that assimilation and deculturation are vital processes and negative facts of Jewish life that must be admitted, recognized, lived with, and contained suffuses their articles. But also, there is the vitalizing spark of the life-force of Judaism, and its understanding, appreciation, and implementation by Jewishly conscious and informed social welfare professionals, working positively in the ambience of a "Jewish" Jewish social welfare agency, that underscores the fact that regeneration, renascence, creativity, growth, and the healing and reintegration of human beings is also an often achieved goal.

Throughout, there is affirmation. The criticism that philanthropy has been substituted for learning and cultural or religious expression is refuted by the high quality of Jewish scholarship and learning related to the professional social work disciplines by distinguished experts that is evident in these papers. Distilled from these essays is the affirmation that this is not philanthropy for its own sake, but is solidly based on a philosophy of relating those ethical principles and spiritual qualities of prophetic, talmudic, and rabbinic Judaism to American life which have given this nation so much of its spiritual stature in civilization.

The new directions that are pointed to, reflect the consensus of the authors that there is significant actual and potential expression for creative American Jewish life to surmount the pressures, trials, and broils of living today, and to heal the inevitable walking wounded that are casualties of the battle. There is, furthermore, the assurance that the thesis of the Commission on Synagogue Relations—that Jewish social, health, and welfare agencies should be Jewish—is the valid and imperative answer to why a "Jewish" agency. In this regard these men, who have earned positions of stature in their professions, make apparent the fact that the level of understanding of Jewishness and the competence to relate and adapt it to the medical and social work disciplines in dealing with human personalities and their problems, are vital prognostic and therapeutic aids in dealing with the neurotic, the psychotic, the alienated, the disaffiliated, and the troubled of our society.

As seen here, the metropolitan urban Jewish community is in ferment and in transition. Allegiances, practices, and forms are changing. The next generation will disclose whether the unique Jewish communal experiment in the history of Diaspora, as highlighted by metropolitan New York and its pioneering and pace-setting Federation of Jewish Philanthropies, will result in a mutation of distinct American Jewish forms, concepts, and expressions as the result of the amalgam on the one hand of new social, economic, political, religious, and intellectual pressures, and on the other the new positive *shiduch* between Judaism and its lay and religious leaders and the social, health, and welfare professionals whose understanding *shadchan* has been the Commission on Synagogue Relations under its brilliant and dedicated director Rabbi Isaac Trainin.

These essays provide authoritative insight into the problems that beset Jews in their individual, family, and community life. This is essential knowledge and understanding for lay and professional communal leaders concerned with the future of Jewish life, who have the responsibility of making wise community social, health, and welfare decisions for future Jewish life in the next third of a century.

DR. JACOB FREID

Contents

11

Judaism and the Community

1

Judaism and Community Relations

On the broad horizon of the Jewish community stand many problems which, as yet, remain unanswered. How do you serve the positive and important needs of the youth of a Hassidic community which is suspicious of, and hostile to, your YM and YWHA? Are there specific Jewish problems in the growing dilemma of family desertion? What shall be the community's response to the desire of Negro Jews to become integrated into the Jewish community? What are the reciprocal "Jewish" obligations of the community and its communal workers to each other?

During the 1930's many of our Jewish youth left the faith and community of their fathers for the false Messiah of the Soviet Internationale. To many the community centers were unable to transmit an intelligible, meaningful rationale for Jewish life. How remarkable it is then to have an example of Murray Gunner's fascinating study, verging on cultural anthropology in a warm Jewish agency setting.

15

Mr. Gunner details how prescient, understanding, sympathetic, and highly capable Jewish community professionals can establish rapport with—as a basis for vital service to—the Hassidim of Williamsburg. It is an intriguing recounting, replete with insights, of the way in which this successful YM and YWHA operation was carried out to its heartwarming result.

Sanford Solender sets forth the way in which the synagogue and the "Y" complement one another to serve American Jewry and to nurture vital and creative Jewish living, both religiously and culturally. Mutual understanding of, and regard for, their respective contributions is necessary if the community truly is to benefit.

Jacob Zuckerman relates how the Family Location Service has helped Jewish families not only in greater New York, but throughout the United States in cases of desertion. He cites interesting cases from his agency's files to prove that there are specific Jewish problems in family desertion.

Rabbi Irving Block depicts the vital, throbbing young Negro Jews of New York City as zealous for more religious education. He calls upon the Jewish community to help these youths achieve that goal. Mr. Benari presents a moving, evocative account, and a plea for integration of The Black Jews into the Brotherhood of the American Jewish community.

Professor Moshe Zucker presents the answer of Jewish tradition and law concerning the mutual responsibilities that exist between the communal servant and the community. His scholarship culls from the Talmud, the Torah, Pirke Avoth, and the sages of Jewish history for their vital judicious and ethical precepts in regard to the proper communal attitude towards collective bargaining, strikes, the treatment and rights of workers, and the obligations of both the community and its servants to each other.

THE PROFESSIONAL PRACTICES AND PRINCIPLES IN HELPING
THE HASSIDIM USE A JEWISH CENTER
by
Murray Gunner, Executive Director, YM and YWHA
of Williamsburg

How would you like to work in a neighborhood where a
great percentage of the Jewish people would do everything
to avoid you and your agency? They would spit on the side-
walk of your agency; they would walk on the other side of
the street to be as far from your agency as possible; or they
would avoid you when you would attempt to speak to them
or their children.

How would you like to work in a neighborhood where one
group of Jewish people picket the stores of other Jewish pro-
prietors, who are open on the Sabbath or other Jewish holidays,
and regard all Jews different from themselves, as *goyim* and
assimilationists?

How would you like to work for an agency where children
of certain *yeshivoths* are threatened with excommunication if
they would set foot in the "Y?"

How would you like to work for an agency where the
holding of hands by the senior adult group is looked upon by
this group of Jewish people as sacriligious, where any socializa-
tion by teenagers is referred to as "Godless," where the youth
lounge, which has pool tables and rock and roll music, is
considered to be a den of iniquity?

How would you like to work in an agency where a rabbi
phones you to complain that one of his girl students, who is
taking a violin lesson at the "Y," was given this lesson in a
room adjoining a boy's class? He was extremely concerned
that this girl may be approached and spoken to by a boy of
the other class.

How would you like to work in an agency where one of the

rabbis indicates to you that he would have no objection to his group of youngsters participating in our physical education activities, but frankly prohibits their admission for fear that they may like other activities of the "Y," feeling this may result in a reduction of his influence on the sect?

How would you like to work at a "Y" where some of the Hassidim of the area indicate that they would have more trust in a YMCA, than a YMHA, because of their fear of dilution of their values by contact with non-Hassidic Jewish people?

How would you like to work in an agency where your offer to help the graduates or seniors of a Hassidic girls' seminary to obtain *shomer shabbos* employment (which they badly need) is rejected by the school principal because he feels the "Y" cannot be trusted?

This is the kind of environment and atmosphere which confronted the Board of Directors and professional staff of the Williamsburg "Y" several years ago . . . and to some extent, exists presently. Who are these people who have made these demands? Where do they come from? How long have they been living in the Williamsburg area, which is the neighborhood the "Y" serves? What do they expect? This is what a professional would ask of any group, whom we would like to serve. He would want to know about their background, their needs, and their culture. Such understanding is essential in establishing a meaningful relationship.

These Hassidic people came to New York City primarily from Hungary and Eastern Europe, and settled in the Williamsburg area in the 1940's. The language spoken by these people is primarily Yiddish and Hungarian. The men and boys wear *payes*; you find a predominance of men, with beards, wearing their long black coats and black hats. You notice also that the men and boys wear *tzitzis*. You rarely see any social contact between their teenage boys and girls. You find women wearing stockings and long sleeves even in very hot weather. When you visit their homes you rarely find a TV set there. You learn that attendance at a movie is quite rare. Their average family has five to seven children. The highest status is accorded to the most learned and to the most observant. Their food habits, holidays, and prayers are far stricter and more intense than the orthodox group.

The spirit of the Jewish holiday is part of life itself. The holiday music, dances, and rituals are deeply observed. During *Simchas Torah,* for example, a number of blocks in the Williamsburg area are roped off to permit singing and dancing in the streets; and this, mind you, occurs in the busy thoroughfares of New York City. During *Succoth,* one observes many *succahs,* in the alleys and back yards, and one sees youngsters and oldsters strolling, almost in a parade-like fashion, with *lulovim* and *esrogim.*

The challenge to the professional staff is how to persuade such a group, having such a "culture," to accept an agency such as a YM and YWHA. How can we influence this group to try our program and to trust us in this process? How can we impress upon this group that our objective is to provide for them activities and facilities which they would consider as desirable, but which they would be unable to obtain through their own institutions and facilities? What can you do to convince them that an agency which has been identified in their minds as essentially sacriligious and assimilationist can be changed to one which, for them, professes respect for their ways and shows a dedication and belief in "Torah-learning?" How do we develop a dialogue with them? Where do we search out people who would be acceptable to them to be our "spokesman" and to help develop some communication between ourselves? How do we convince them that their belief —that the majority of our Board of Directors and Federation

of Jewish Philanthropies' Board of Directors, wants them to
change their way of life — is not so?

What were the professional techniques used to develop a
relationship with them? Our first task was to contact people
in the community who were, in some way, accepting the "Y's"
purposes and functions and who also had the respect and
confidence of the Hassidim. The rabbinical consultant, and the
consultant on "Ys" and Camps of Federation of Jewish
Philanthropies were most helpful in bringing about meaningful
contacts, as well as the rabbi of the neighborhood Young
Israel. Also a key person in the community, respected by
the Hassidim, was a physician who has a very large Hassidic practice. (He, incidentally, is an honorary president of
our Board of Directors.) He referred many of his patients to
the "Y" for medical reasons — suggesting gym and swimming
pool activities, for children and adults, or nursery school for
certain children. To accommodate these referrals, we appointed
to our staff rabbis who had lived in the area and who had
relationships and contacts with these Hassidic people. We made
sure that our secretarial staff had knowledge of Yiddish and
could easily and fluently speak the language. We sent out
literature in English and Yiddish. Our posters were made up
bilingually.

As we met with these Hassidim, we learned the conditions
that would be required for any of them to set foot in the "Y."
There could be no mixed (boys and girls) swimming or mixed
athletics or mixed groups in any of the other classes. The
instructors would have to be essentially people from the
Yeshivoth, or people who respect and understand them. Our
schedules would have to dovetail in with the *Yeshivoth*
schedules, and the content of the activity in which they partici-
pated would have to be acceptable to them. These criteria
evolved after a number of teas were held in their homes, in

the "Y," at the PTA, or anywhere that we were able to informally talk with them—in their restaurants, in their stores, or in the streets. We took the initiative in these contacts. We did not wait for them to come in. We took rejection in stride; if one person or group or rabbi rejected us, we contacted the next person or group. We did not veer from our objectives, despite many disappointments, because we felt our objectives to be sound. And this is essential for a professional : he must have strong dedication and conviction in his cause. He must be a doer besides an enabler. He must proceed aggressively at times, and passively on other occasions, but always with great sensitivity.

The program developed as we perceived it. We professionals walked around our neighborhood with our eyes and ears open. We went to their synagogue and prayed with them. We shopped in the same stores as they shopped. We ate in the same restaurants. We read the newspapers they read. We observed that some of the people could not speak English well, so we set up English classes for them. When we observed that some of the children were wearing clothes that did not fit them very well, we encouraged their mothers to take sewing classes, and we bought sewing machines for the class. Some of the children were having difficulty in English subjects in the *Yeshivoth*, so we set up tutoring classes for them. Some of the people had a latent interest in art by virtue of what we discovered in our home visits, and we developed an art class for them. We were concerned that the youngsters had long study schedules in the *Yeshivoth* with very little physical exercise, so we developed a physical education program for them. We developed posture and modern dance instruction to improve their co-ordination and their physical agility. We learned that many of the people were having difficulty in making ends meet, so we started a program in conjunction with the Federation Employment and Guidance Service to obtain *Shomer Shabbos* jobs for them. We were concerned that some of them had medical problems, child welfare problems, and family problems, so we developed a referral service to the proper agencies. And, where the social workers had some trouble understanding them, we advised the social workers of the Hassidic values, so that they would be able to serve the family more effectively. When we learned that a number of women wanted to relax from their daily cares, we developed a Homemakers' Holiday so that the women could participate in gym, swim, and steam-room activities. In this program we set up a baby-sitting service for their children and we also served lunch for the entire group.

We observed, in the neighborhood, that the driving habits of some of the Hassidim could be improved, so we set up driver education courses for the neighborhood and enrolled over eighty for this course. (We were thinking of having this course in our auditorium with the men separated from the women by a curtain. But we were cautioned that some of the boys and girls might socialize at the end of the evening, so we set up two different classes on different days to avoid any problems.)

In addition, the Williamsburg "Y" developed a camp for Hassidic boys because of their great need for some desirable and appropriate activity in the summer time. They used to sit on the stoops of the hot city streets. We wanted them to be in a countrified atmosphere where they would have fresh air, water, sports, arts and crafts, pioneering, in addition to their Torah learning and *glat* kosher food. In order to develop competent staff for this camp, we set up a series of camp training sessions for the Hassidim. Sixty individuals have, so far, been trained, thereby providing a reservoir of Hassidim versed in camping.

Because of the great success of this Hassidic boys camp, called Camp Mogen Avraham, the "Y" was besieged with urgent demands for a similar camp for girls. The "Y" purchased a campsite for Hassidic girls and operated it for the first time in 1965. The camp is called the Dr. H. Melmuth Sternberg Camp and is located at the Max H. Sklar Campgrounds in the Catskill Mountains.

So the development of the program for the Hassidim expanded to include karate, life saving, judo, weight lifting, fencing, basketball, modern dance, cooking, sewing, woodworking, nursery programs, science, etc. These activities were all based on the needs we learned of, from contacts with these people. In order to accommodate their needs our elementary school program, which originally had been in the afternoon as in most other "Y's," was shifted to the early evening and Sunday because these youngsters attended *Yeshivoth* up until 6 :00 P.M. Our food program, which was kosher, was changed to *glat* kosher in our nurseries and our camps. (*Glat* kosher is a higher form of *kashruth* and also is more expensive.) For those children who, for various reasons, had to remain in the city during the summer, a Hassidic day camp in the "Y" was developed with Torah learning, *Yeshivoth* staff and a full complement of regular day-camp activities. Room schedules and use of areas of the building had to be modified to accommodate this new camp and groups.

The development of program for a group is based on the professional's knowledge of the "potential" needs of the group and of the "expressed" requests by the group. The professional must be willing to search into every possible need, interest, or desire of the individual and, if it fits into the overall agency function and purpose, try to convince the person that the "Y's" proposed service is most desirable for his welfare. The professional has to be a good salesman. His product is program. His aim is not to make a monetary profit but to provide service for the person's benefit as defined by the agency goals. The professional knows that every individual has many needs and that the potential area of service to this individual is substantial. The challenge to the professional social worker is clear. William E. Gordon, in his "Critique of the Working Definition of Social Work," in the *Social Work Publication* of October, 1962, states that "Social Work practice is interventive action directed to purposes and guided by the values, knowledge, and techniques which are collectively unique, acknowledged by, and identified with the social work profession."

What are some of the problems our staff faced? Some of our professional staff with non-orthodox orientation and background had to learn about special Hassidic customs and had to adjust to new realities when working with this group. We had to depend on our rabbinical staff for much of this information. We had to obtain from them information as to who were the status leaders of the Hassidic individuals we were serving. Let me give you an example :

We observed that during the seven-week period between Passover and *Shevuoth* holidays there was a severe drop in attendance in the modern dance and music classes. We learned that during this *S'fira* period parents were reluctant to send their children to activities which incorporated music in its program. We learned, too, that if we obtained approval from an acceptable prominent rabbi, the parents would be willing to send their children to the activities. This rabbi was consulted and when we explained that the music was basically instructional in content rather than for enjoyment in purpose, he indicated that in his opinion, our program did not violate the spirit of the *S'fira*. We then advised these parents of this rabbi's opinion. Most of the children came back to class the following week. Another instance of our dependence on our rabbis was an occasion when a group of Yeshiva boys came to our "Y" for their first swimming program. The boys were all set to go into the water with their *yarmulkas* and *tzitzas* on. I did not feel qualified to tell them to take them off. I had to call our rabbi on our staff to make this decision. What we tried to develop was productive teamwork between the rabbis and the social worker. The rabbi helped the professional social worker in providing the guidelines for serving the Hassidim. In turn, the professional social worker imparted knowledge of social work techniques and disciplines to the rabbi.

We found too that it was important to identify with the values of the parents, rather than those of their children (who in some cases, wanted to rebel) if the Hassidim were to have confidence in us. When several of their teenage girls wanted to participate in a "Y" Saturday night teenage dance, we stopped them at the door and advised them that they could not participate unless they had permission from their parents. When several elementary school girls completed their Sunday afternoon modern dance class, and were attracted by the rock and roll rhythms of the teenage lounge, a number of them, fascinated by this rhythm, went into the teenage lounge with intent on "twisting" with the others in the group. Our rabbi, observing this, asked them to leave inasmuch as their parents, in his opinion, would not condone such behavior. When we have Hassidic teenagers coming to us asking guidance about going to secular college, we indicate to them that we would want their parents' permission to discuss this matter with them, because the practice of most of the Hassidic groups is to discourage their youth from participating in secular colleges for their advanced learning.

If we want to serve Hassidim, we must know what is acceptable and what is not acceptable to them. When we were searching for a campsite for Hassidic girls, we had to bear in mind that their place for swimming had to be private, because we learned that it was not proper for the girls to be seen by men or boys in bathing suits. The Hassidim look askance at the "Coney Island" type of atmosphere, whereby boys and girls

walk around in a rather "exposed" manner. So we had to look
for a campsite with a private lake or swimming pool which had
complete privacy from the outside; and this was a sizeable
handicap to overcome !

I'm sure that a professional social worker in working with
a group would, where appropriate and feasible, try to help
improve the living conditions of his group. (This process certainly strengthens relationships between the agency and the
group.) The Board and staff of the agency made every effort
to obtain improved and suitable housing for the Hassidim.
When the city was developing housing projects in the area,
representatives of our agency were one of the groups interpreting to the City Housing Authority the desirability of
installing what is called a "Shabbos elevator." In such an
elevator, one need not push the button to activate it. The
elevator, during Sabbath or other holidays, moves automatically and continuously, stopping at each floor. This is
acceptable to many of the Hassidim because, even though you
are moving up and down, it is reasoned that technically you are
standing still in one place, because there is no horizontal travel.

The question has often arisen as to the relationship between
the Hassidic and non-Hassidic groups. Originally, there was
tremendous resistance on the part of the Hassid to accept the
non-Hassid. The Hassid tended to look down on the non-
Hassid. The Hassid used to react quite emotionally in his
distaste for the non-Hassid. The non-Hassid did not expect
such a negative reaction, so their response was one of disdain
and hostility. In this last year though, we have observed a
leveling off of these reactions. The Hassid seems now to tolerate
the non-Hassid. His reaction is more non-violent. The non-
Hassid also is somewhat more tolerant of the Hassid. Their
dialogue at the moment seems to be a distant respect for each
other, as, "Hello," or "Good-bye," or some other courteous
remark. We have found that in our agency Sports Night, where

the Hassid and non-Hassid participate, a number of Hassidim have won awards and were applauded by the *total* audience. We find that in activities of *movement,* such as basketball, roller-skating, and swimming, the Hassid and the non-Hassid inter-mingle. However, where you take a *sedentary* activity, as in sewing, the Hassidic and non-Hassidic children divide them-selves each week on opposite sides of the room. We also can report that though at one time the Hassidic parents used to strongly resent a non-Hassidic child in the same class with their children, such resistance has decreased considerably. The staff, however, has to move with great caution and sensitivity in this area.

When I spoke to one Hassidic rabbi about encouraging a dialogue between some of their teenagers and our non-Hassidic teenagers, this rabbi indicated that he would not expose his teenagers to our "godless" group. However, this opinion was not shared by another rabbi of a more liberal Hassidic sect. He was willing to develop such a dialogue. (This rabbi is also experimenting by sending six of his top teenagers to a secular college, with the hope that after the completion of this secular education, they would return to the Hassidic fold with their newly acquired skills.)

We have involved some of the Hassidic teenagers in writing a summary of the *Sedra* of the week. This *Sedra* is posted on the bulletin board for all to read. We have involved some of the Hassidic girls with the non-Hassidic girls in decorating the "Y" with flowers and Jewish holiday exhibits. Our hope is that the non-Hassidic will learn from the Hassid in Jewish matters. But, many a Hassid is fearful that the Hassid teenagers will learn the "undesirable" ways of life of the non-Hassid. So a dialogue will be a slow process! It is constantly being resisted by a number of individuals from the very conservative Hassidic sects. The relationship will more likely begin to develop between the more *liberal* Hassidic sects and the non-Hassidic individuals.

My impression is that on the overall basis, where these people have been at the "Y" for close on two years, there is a mellowing process going on. I recall that there used to be fun made by the non-Hassidic individuals of the boys with *payes,* and the men with their black garb. It is taken more for granted now; people get accustomed to it, and one hears much less criticism of such differences now.

A number of problems arise with both Hassidic and non-Hassidic groups under one roof. Our rabbinical staff had to feel comfortable in working with the non-Hassidic groups —and this is not easy. (And, may I add, that our rabbis have to face, frequently, the wrath of some Hassidic rabbis, who state they have sold their principles by working at the "Y.") Problems also arise when non-Hassidic parents bring in their children to register for one of our non-Hassidic camps but, when they observe the boys with *payes* in the lobby, they withdraw their children, stating that this is not the kind of environment that they want for their offspring. We have had instances where the non-Hassidic parents complain about the intensity of Jewish programming and we have been asked to "secularize" the program more.

We have had problems relating to the use of the gym and other facilities. For instance, whenever we have the Hassidic boys using the gym (with other non-Hassidic boys), the presence of the Hassidic boys makes it prohibitive for the girls to be in the spectator's gallery. Our athletic staff trained a cheer-leader squad of girls to cheer at all games. This group of girls resents not performing at some of the agency functions and games because Hassidic boys are present. The professional has to constantly interpret, to each group, the reason for the limitations. This is what the professionals of all agencies are required to do whenever there is a conflict of limitation of time, use, and participation in activities and facilities. The rabbi had to defer to a non-orthodox staff member to do this interpretation.

We have three country camps and three day camps under the auspices of the Williamsburg "Y." In one of our orthodox camps, which is non-Hassidic — Camp Hatikvah — we have to be extremely careful that the staff we hire is able to work with *co-ed* activities and in an atmosphere less religious than in the Hassidic camp of Mogen Avraham, or of The Dr. H. Melmuth Sternberg camp. One has to be aware that the different departments and camps of the "Y" require different kinds of staff, depending on the clientele that is to be served, whether Hassidic or non-Hassidic, and on the special needs of each group. We have to be extremely careful that we do not impose Hassidic standards on the non-Hassidic group, just as we do not impose or encourage any non-Hassidic standards on the Hassid.

The "Y" has been able to attract, within the last two years, 1,400 Hassidim to its program. They are still increasing in numbers because of the satisfactory experience that they are having. They are bringing in their friends and members of their family. We are constantly expanding our activities to meet their interests. At the same time, we are continuing to serve about 1,800 non-Hassidim. These are the two different worlds we at the "Y" work with, at the same time — under one roof.

Our staff, in working with the Hassidim, uses the same generic principles as in working with any other resistant client group. The worker has to familiarize himself with the client group's needs, customs, sensitivities, likes, dislikes, and their leaders and institutions. He has to develop conditions which make for a beginning relationship. If he, personally, is not acceptable to the client, an intermediary more acceptable must be acquired to make the necessary contacts and to act as an intermediary. The professional does not prejudge or criticize the clients' mores. He makes no demands, requests, or innuendos indicating that he wants them to change. He accepts them where they are and treats them with dignity and respect. He listens to them sincerely and with dedication to serve them. He accepts their resistances and their rejections with understanding. He does research, he studies their literature, and he consults with their representatives and teachers to clarify such practices and procedures. He sets up the necessary atmosphere, appropriate staff, program content, and flexible schedules to meet his clients' interests. Interestingly enough, in this whole process, our non-Hassidic staff, in their study of the Hassid, has strengthened their information and Jewish knowledge and has been greatly stimulated to search more deeply into the Jewish traditional history and folklore. We believe we have become more knowledgeable and have developed increased pride in our Jewish heritage in the process.

The essential principle is the ability of the professional to develop a process whereby the people, group, or individual whom he desires to serve, is helped to accept such service in a manner in which the individual or group retains his status and at the same time is helped and benefits thereby.

The professional has to develop the ability of learning how to ferret out the need of an individual; of finding the proper key where their resistances can be unlocked and then fitted into the agency function and goals. As an example, when, in my visit to one Hassidic family I made no headway in trying to persuade them to utilize the "Y," I, in leaving, noticed a group of paintings on their wall. I remarked that the paintings were beautifully done and inquired as to who did them. The lady of the house for the first time smiled and said that she did them. In searching for the key to bring her closer to the agency, I asked her whether she would be willing to honor us by exhibiting her paintings at the "Y." She said she would be delighted to do so. With this beginning she also obtained for us exhibits of ten of her Hassidic friends. The exhibit was extremely successful. We then contacted the instructor of art of most of these women. He was a *Cubaritcha* rabbi. He agreed to become the "Y" art instructor. This class has grown and has put on a number of outdoor Hassidic exhibits which have attracted many people.

In many communities, professionals find groups or individuals who are hostile to the "Y" for a variety of reasons. For instance, in one community in which I accepted employment, I learned that the synagogues and the adult Jewish organizations did not want to accept the "Y" because they felt threatened that this newly developed "Y" would "pirate" their leadership, membership, and funds. Our goals then were to develop a relationship with them whereby we could show them that the "Y" could strengthen, not weaken, their organizations. After several months of meeting with various presidents and leadership of synagogues and adult organizations, we learned that they had similar problems in common (in different degrees), in areas of declining membership, poor programs, difficulty in obtaining financial support, poor public relations, drop in attendance, etc.

In order to acquire this information, it was necessary for members of the staff to meet with these people, either in their home, their place of business, or other suitable place convenient to the leader of the adult organizations, and this took several months.

Eventually they became convinced that the "Y" could help them with their problems and the "Y" then developed an Adult Leadership Training Program for Jewish adult organizations with the "Y" acting as the administrator and coordinator.

In regard to the rabbis, one refused to even see me. I tried to approach his president, but he also said that he didn't want anything to do with the "Y" executive. I learned that the President attended services every Friday evening. I made it my business to visit his synagogue each Friday evening for services and eventually we were able to talk about the problems relating between the synagogue and the "Y." The result was that I was given the opportunity to speak before their Board of Directors to indicate the areas where the "Y" and the synagogue could jointly work together. Having learned of their need for a dramatics and recreation leader, we offered to supply one of our instructors for the synagogue for several months on a part-time basis. The following year the other rabbi asked for a similar arrangement.

The result of both of these approaches was that the synagogues and organizations were persuaded that they could be helped by utilizing the resources of the "Y." In this helpful and strengthening process the "Y" gained the confidence of these leaders and, together, they increased and improved the services of the community. This process is not an easy one. The professional faces many resistances on the part of different individuals and groups. His function is to work with these resistances and hopefully to decrease them.

The community, neighborhood, and the respective organizations all benefit from this interventive action and helpful approach. This approach works when the groups or individuals you desire to serve feel they are being helped and strengthened by this service. Your agency also benefits because it is accomplishing its stated goals and purposes. This process of strengthening and helping groups and individuals must be a never-ending one. It must never cease. The professional must constantly recruit new members and develop new services within the limits, of course, of the size of the agency facility, budget, and staff. There is always erosion and dropouts in membership, and a tiring of the "same old program." One must keep ahead of this inevitable process.

I am often asked: "What advice would you give to other

"Y's" who may become involved with this element?" I would say this by way of answer:

It is important that there is a person or people on full time staff, or as consultants, who are of the ultra-orthodox. It is important that the other staff members are sensitive to what the ultra-orthodox want and do not make judgments as to the validity of the ultra-orthodox way of life. The professional has to accept the individual and the group where they are and to provide for this group the kind of activities which they desire, and which are in accordance with the philosophy and objectives of the "Y."

It is important that the "Y," in every way possible, show respect and sensitivity to the religious beliefs of the ultra-orthodox. For instance, this year we closed for the first time on the eve of *Tisha B'av*. We also did not serve any meat in our five camp operations on *Tisha B'av* and did not have any swimming that day either. At Camp Mogen Avraham, meat was not served nor swimming permitted for the nine-day period prior to *Tisha B'av*.

Our Saturday night programs start at least one hour after dark. We close early on Friday and on the eve of most of the important Jewish holidays.

Certain requests made by the ultra-orthodox have to be denied. For instance, they asked the "Y" to close on Purim, in the early afternoon, because it is a family holiday and members of the family should get together then. We indicated, that those ultra-orthodox who desired to leave early could do so, but we did not want to deprive the non-orthodox, of the use of the "Y," at that time.

Each request made by the ultra-orthodox or by the other Jewish groups or individuals, has to be carefully studied for its effects on each — and for its consonance with "Y" objectives — before a decision is made. Our approach this past year has so far shown good results. This past year we enrolled 1,500 *new* members — ultra-orthodox and non-orthodox — in the Williamsburg "Y." We already were advised by another sect, that they are interested in exploring with us, our providing activities for their youngsters.

We at the "Y" must be constantly on the alert to help wherever possible and for people to have confidence in our objectives and sincerity. For instance, when we heard of one sect being dispossessed from their quarters, we immediately offered the facilities of our "Y." This example, plus other instances of "Y" considerateness, has gone a long way to inspire confidence in the agency.

I should add, too, that the use of professional knowledge, techniques, and discipline is most helpful and necessary in our task. They must be applied with common sense and flexibility.

The professional must also trust his "healthy" and "normal" instincts where no written or previous guide is available, feel free to experiment and create . . . and not get discouraged too quickly. This recipe is bound to lead you to the right track. Why don't you try it?

THE SYNAGOGUE AND THE "Y"
by
Sanford Solendar
Executive Vice President, National Jewish Welfare Board

As Jewish life in America has unfolded, various Jewish institutions have emerged in response to the needs of the Jew in this free land. Any reasoned consideration of the relationship of the synagogue and the Young Men's and Young Women's Hebrew Association, frequently known as "Jewish Community Center," must start with the recognition that each of these institutions is firmly rooted in this American experience. Each has assumed the special character prompted by the necessities of life on these shores. Each fulfills a distinctive purpose and receives community support because it plays a significant part in our group life.

Our understanding of the relationship of these two institutions will be grounded soundly if there is appreciation of the particular competence and the unique contribution of each. Several generalizations appropriately precede such a definition for the YM and YWHA. First, the "Y" is an institution deeply committed to broad, integrated Jewish and general purposes. Its *raison d'être* is advancing the fulfillment and richness of the lives of individual Jews, the quality of our group and communal existence, and the effectiveness of our contribution to the larger democratic society. Broadly speaking, the "Y's" purposes are similar to those of the synagogue. The distinction between the "Y" and the synagogue is primarily in the *way* in which each contributes to these goals.

Second, the Jewish group today, as in the past, is influenced by the mores of the current milieu. Our complex, changing society characteristically has developed institutions with specialized purposes and with personnel having competence to implement these functions. It is commonly accepted that particular institutions meet definable aspects of community need. The vibrance of community life generally depends upon the vitality of a complex of institutions — among them being the school, the hospital, the library, the church or synagogue, and the recreation center. The quality of our life as Jews is conditioned by the level of achievement of *each* of the institutions devoted to enriching our experience as a people.

We have come far from the elementary stage in which it was assumed that every organization should engage in every program needed by those it serves. The need for case work by counsellees of a vocational service agency does not warrant its taking on the family agency's function any more than the

interest of "Y" members in religious worship calls for the
conduct of a synagogue by the "Y." The development of
institutions dedicated to given functions and possessing
specialized skills for their conduct is a strength in our social
structure.

This assertion of the integrity of discrete institutions as a
safeguard of the quality of community services must not be
misunderstood to be a case for the preservation of institutions
for their own sake. Traditional institutions which become
obsolete must be modified or eliminated as circumstances
require. Institutions always must meet the test of contempor-
aneous relevance and viability.

Third, close inter-relationship of these complementary
institutions is essential for the best service to people. This is
achievable by effective collaboration between them, rather than
by merging all functions into a single entity with the loss of
the unique contributions of each. The important challenge
today in Jewish life is to achieve mutual understanding and
respect between all Jewish institutions, as the basis for their
cooperation in behalf of the goals they share in meeting
Jewish needs.

These principles have direct application to the relationship
of the synagogue and the "Y." This relationship has potentialities for great good in American Jewish life, which can be
realized only if each sees the other as having distinct purposes, which, when mutually strengthened and rendered
cooperatively, produce a finer community existence.

What then is the particular contribution of the YM and
YWHA?

First, fundamental to the "Y" is appreciation of the fact that
association between people in groups has inherent learning
and growth values which are influential development forces
in the lives of participants. With skilled leadership this
experience can be a dominant and positive element for them.

Participation in Jewish group experience affords the opportunity for growth through Jewish association, not only in broad areas which affect all persons, but in relation to the need for Jewish identification, understanding of the meaning of Jewishness, vital Jewish living, and significant Jewish communal participation.

At the heart of the "Y's" uniqueness is recognition of this profound educational significance of Jewish group association. The voluntary Jewish groupings through which people give greater meaning to their expanding leisure and satisfy their needs for rewarding social relationships, and recreation, become for the "Y" a powerful fountainhead for human growth and for helping Jews to enrich their Jewishness. The distinguishing function of the "Y" is the provision of the elements and resources needed to release these potentialities for the benefit of individuals, groups, and the community. This understanding of the values of human association and this commitment to their use for positive Jewish and general purposes distinguishes the "Y" from other institutions which strive for the same broad objectives, but utilize other means. The "Y" views such use of people's Jewish group living as having *intrinsic* value for those who participate. It differs substantially from many other organizations, which consider Jewish group association primarily as an instrument for retaining the affiliation of persons so that they may be induced to participate in other primary programs fostered by the sponsor.

Basic to the achievement of these purposes by the "Y" is its use of the best equipped professional competence for work with people in groups for socially desirable ends. Social work, and particularly its social group work specialization, is the profession through which the "Y" serves Jewish groups and releases the growth potentialities which are inherent in Jewish group association. The relationships of such skilled "Y" staff, and the leaders they guide, with Jewish persons and groups are the fertile soil in which personal, group, and community growth is nurtured and Jewish living is made more creative.

Social work, applied with the added knowledge and competency for its utilization in relation to Jewish purposes, is the core of professional practice in the "Y" and permeates its staff structure. This is true equally of the staff working directly with groups and on the executive and supervisory level, who are chosen because of their social work experience and their ability to lead and supervise the entire agency process.

Social work is not the only profession employed in the "Y." Adult education, pre-school teaching, health and physical education, and others have significant places in the organization. The central fact, however, is that social work is the professional foundation of the "Y" — the context within which it functions.

Since the crux of the "Y's" work is constructive use of Jewish group association, and because program is the vehicle for this, the more complete the program of group activity the more effective the results. The fact that such programming is primary in the "Y" enables it to give full sway to a wide scope of activity, from friendship groups, to interest groups, to mass activities. The close inter-relationship of the "Y's" many activities fosters mobility of members from one activity to another as interests vary or expand, and to combinations of activities which can enrich human associations. The breadth of Jewish concerns in the programs of informal, voluntary "Y" groups can offer a unique opportunity for Jewish experience, often exceeding that of the formal educational program.

Fundamental to the "Y" is its non-doctrinal approach with individuals. Committed to broad, inclusive Jewish interests and not confined to a particular Jewish religious denomination or ideology, the "Y" can introduce persons to a range of Jewish concerns. Its freedom from the obligation to use group experience to fortify membership adherence to a given doctrine or viewpoint, places the "Y" in a strong position to facilitate the creative development of individuals through group experience. Such permissiveness is basic to the "Y's" atmosphere and way of work. While representing definite American and Jewish ideals, the "Y's" staff can encourage members to find their way to those aspects of Jewish life and general citizenship which best meet their needs.

An understanding that specialized facilities are essential for productive group work services is another important "Y" characteristic. Lounges, game rooms, health and physical education areas, special interest workshops (especially in the arts), mass activity areas, outdoor facilities, and camping resources are the settings for such programs. The "Y's" facilities are adapted to the special needs of this program and are administered to achieve the desired values. The group work program has priority in the use of these facilities. They are available for planned future use, to an extent usually impossible in institutions which house such programs but must give first call to other activities.

The "Y" encourages relaxed, informal conduct in its facilities, tending to free people for creative social experience. This contrasts with the frequent situation in other organizations—notably synagogues—where the attitude toward behavior, and the concern for preserving physical appointments for highly formal occasions, often results in considerable restrictions, especially upon youth participants.

The "Y's" distinctiveness is further reflected in the way its operational practices are molded to its central concern for Jewish group experience. A variety of closely related agency practices are designed to accommodate the needs of a program of group association. For example, the "Y's" membership admission system interprets the "Y's" purposes and program to applicants and secures information which will support the best service for them. The records of group activities and member participation, like the provisions for clerical resources, are geared to the needs of the "Y" program. Such practices are built into the organization. That is why a "Y" program cannot be grafted successfully on to an organization with other primary purposes. This program can prosper only in an institution in which services to people with the goals and approach of social work described here is the central purpose.

Its social group work function and competency enables the "Y" to collaborate professionally with other social agencies in the Jewish and general community in behalf of individuals and families requiring special attention. As a social work agency, the "Y" is equipped for a partnership in service with other agencies similarly manned, thus providing a resource in depth for meeting such needs.

The second aspect of the "Y's" distinctiveness is the community quality of its purpose, structure, and program. Here is an organization in which individuals from all segments of the Jewish community join in group activities. Persons of every age from all the religious denominations, and those not affiliated religiously, participate in "Y" groups. A cross-section of economic and social levels usually is found in the "Y." Such inclusiveness produces a replica of the Jewish community, enabling the "Y" to provide a peculiarly community-type experience for its members, who by joining the "Y" in effect associate themselves with the Jewish community. Not only is the "Y" membership representative, but the Board reflects most community segments.

The "Y's" community nature is articulated also through the obligations it assumes to the Federation or other central Jewish body. The "Y" is an integral part of the Jewish communal services family and has a straight line of responsibility to the total Jewish community through the Federation. The community character of the "Y" explains the appropriateness of its being a recipient of support from Jewish communal sources and from Community Chests.

It is worthy of note that Community Chest type of funds are supplied to sectarian services only through social agencies such as "Y's," and not through churches or synagogues. While the wish to avoid supporting proselytizing activities in which churches might engage is a factor in this matter, a major consideration is the preference for the community auspices of social agencies and their primary concern for serving people through social welfare programs utilizing social work. The "Y's" community support also is related to the fact that as an institution of the whole community, the "Y" is obligated to charge fees which are within the reach of the majority of the community. To maintain this principle and provide a program of good quality, the "Y" must receive subsidy from the community.

The communal nature of the "Y" is reflected clearly in its capacity to accommodate both those already affiliated with congregations or other Jewish organizations, and the substantial sector of Jews not connected in an organized way with the Jewish group. It is common knowledge that many regard themselves as Jews but do not find prevailing religious, ideological, or other special-purpose oriented organizations to be an acceptable channel for their Jewish identification. The "Y" is an important link for many of these unaffiliated Jews, often being the most accessible and felicitous threshold through which they can enter into broader Jewish participation. The capacity of the "Y" is to reach out to these people and to relate them to Jewish life is one of its important features.

In short, the whole perspective of the "Y" tends to be "community rather than institutional," and this permeates its concept of membership, program, staff, and structure.

Avenues for Collaboration

As we have said when we talk of the relationship of the synagogue and the "Y," this must be based upon recognition that each performs important Jewish communal functions which are distinctive and different. Assuming a healthy mutual regard for the functions of each, what are some of the approaches by which the two can collaborate effectively in meeting the needs of the Jew?

The first and possibly the most important field for such cooperation is that of intelligent use of each other in meeting the needs of members. How often does a "Y" staff member who discovers that a person may be helped by religious identification and experience communicate with the rabbi of a nearby congregation and arrange for referral of the person to the synagogue? In how many instances does a group worker in a "Y," dealing with a family confronting difficult moral and ethical problems, consider that the synagogue and the rabbi can be a valuable resource for the family? Are there sufficient indications of "Y" workers referring Center members to synagogues for formal Jewish education? Conversely, how frequently does a rabbi who becomes aware of a child's need for healthy group association refer this youngster to a "Y?" How often do rabbis encountering adults with difficulty in establishing Jewish contacts and friendships suggest the "Y" as a source to which the individual can turn? On how many occasions do rabbis or "Y" workers consult with each other about the problem of a family affiliated with both the "Y" and the synagogue?

While evidences of such collaboration occur with increasing frequency, there are too many instances in which this is absent. Basic to this type of cooperation is such appreciation for the functions of the "Y" and its staff on the part of the rabbi, and for the role of the synagogue and the rabbi on the part of the Center worker, that each respects the capacity of the other, translating this into mutual exchange and utilization.

Perhaps the best form of such joint effort is that in which rabbi and "Y" worker help an individual or a family by collaborating over a span of time through sharing information and experience, considering jointly the problems of the person or family, and combining efforts to assist the individual or family in both the synagogue and the "Y." It is not too much to expect such cooperation.

A second form of collaboration is the use of its distinctive competence by the "Y" to aid the synagogue. Synagogues commonly conduct youth programs, such as local affiliates of the National Federation of Temple Youth or the United Synagogue Youth, the purpose of which is to encourage the adherence of the young person to the congregation and his participation in the congregation's religious program. The Center can assist substantially the leaders of such youth groups to carry out these programs more effectively for their logical and appropriate synagogal purposes.

Within the congregation there are various adult groups, such as brotherhoods, sisterhoods, men's or women's leagues, and parents' associations. The "Y" has competence in aiding Jewish organizations to function successfully and can render a valuable service by counselling the officers of synagogue adult groups or the synagogue staff working with these groups.

The "Y" can help the synagogue by taking initiative in sponsoring inter-Jewish-organizational activities such as athletic tournaments, leadership training projects, and major civic events. Sponsorship of such projects on a community basis under the auspices of the "Y" enables groups to engage in activities with other community groups, whether from synagogues and various organizations or from the "Y" itself, thus enriching the experience of all.

The sponsorship of community-wide Jewish cultural projects

by the "Y," such as a Jewish Book Council or a Jewish Music Council, or of major Jewish events, like Jewish Book Month or a memorable Jewish anniversary, affords the "Y" a natural opportunity to serve the synagogues by helping them to work together with other congregations and groups for community purposes.

This cooperation must be a two-way street and there are important forms of aid which the synagogue can render to the "Y." The rabbi can help the "Y" in many important ways. He can be an invaluable resource in staff training and adult education. He can be an important consultant on "Y" program and policy. By offering their facilities for "Y" branches and extension programs, synagogues can assist "Y's" to serve community segments otherwise not reached with "Y" work. The synagogue and the rabbi can interpret the "Y" to the community and gain better understanding, appreciation, and support for it.

Relationships between synagogues and "Y's" have not always been free of problems. Various factors at given times and in particular situations have caused tensions and difficulties. Often the insecurities of developing institutions in the process of obtaining community acceptance and financial support affected the attitudes of both institutions. Personalities inevitably complicated institutional relationships and conflicts between synagogue and "Y," lay or professional leaders have contributed to this situation. There are instances of conflict between the two for time periods in the lives of individuals or for the affiliation of families.

But the task of the Jewish community is vast indeed. There is an enormous unresolved challenge for every Jewish institution today to make the heritage of Jews more significant in their lives: to nurture more vital and creative Jewish living. The synagogue is basic in Jewish life and has a major responsibility for this. The "Y" is an essential Jewish institution especially suited to meeting the modern needs of the Jew. The two complement one another in serving American Jewry. The Jewish community has a right to expect that each understand the other and appreciate their respective contributions. Nothing less than such mutual regard and cooperation can fulfill the expectations of an increasingly mature and vital community.

SOME JEWISH ASPECTS OF FAMILY DESERTION
by
Jacob T. Zukerman
Executive Director and Chief Counsel, Family Location Service

When a Rachel Cohen or Sarah Levy—or give her any other fictitious name—comes to us in the Family Location Service for help in locating her deserting husband, what special problems or needs does she bring with her by virtue of her Jewishness? What special understanding is she likely to expect of us because we are an agency of the Federation of Jewish Philanthropies of New York? The same question might be asked about the request of a similarly fictitious Harry Israel or a Moishe Schwartz—for wives leave home too.

Since the founding of the National Desertion Bureau (our former name) in 1905, some 75,000 families have been made known to us, most of them involving situations in which one of the family members was missing. The great majority of them have been Jewish families to whom we have provided location service, short term casework, and legal aid. From our very creation as a brainchild of the National Conference of Jewish Charities (as it was then known), during the hectic years of Jewish immigration and later during the holocausts and aftermaths of two world wars, we have continued to provide service, in the main, to residents of greater New York. Yet, in a limited, but nevertheless very prominent, way we

have helped families all over the United States and even in
many foreign lands. For, we always have been and still are
the only voluntary non-profit agency in the world specializing
in problems arising out of the very serious phenomenon known
as family desertion.

That it is an increasingly vexing problem can be gleaned
from the fact that there are over 11,000,000 women and
children in the U.S., who are not being adequately supported
by estranged fathers. Last year, almost $950,000,000 was
spent for Aid to Dependent Children in such cases. In New
York City alone, it is estimated that there are 400,000 such
women and children affected by the desertion of the father.

Yet, in spite of the fact that this is certainly no more of a
problem among Jews than non-Jews, we are the only
specialized voluntary agency in the field. In New York City,
we are trying to get other sectarian groups to either provide
such service or to help subsidize an enlarged operation by our
agency which might service non-Jewish cases.

We also operate a service in the Family Courts of Manhattan, Bronx, Brooklyn, and Queens known as the Jewish
Federation Family Court Unit, in which caseworkers help
Jewish families who are referred by either the judges or proba-
tion workers. Here there are problems of custody and visitation
of children, support of aged parents by adult children, short-
term counseling in marital difficulties, and referrals to other
Jewish agencies and institutions. Here our legally oriented
caseworkers have been helping these families to arrive at agreements, whenever possible, without actual court action.

Now what are the specific Jewish problems involved in
many of the cases we handle? (There have been 2,821 new
Jewish cases in the last five years alone. Incidentally, the
overwhelming number of Jewish clients are referred to us by
the courts, legal aid societies, and by lawyers.)

We have many situations involving a *Get*. Mrs. A came to

us, for example, to find Mr. A from whom she had been civilly divorced back in 1955 on the ground of adultery (after we had located him living with another woman). She now wanted to marry Mr. B who insisted upon her getting a religious *Get* from Mr. A. Now we had to find Mr. A a second time. We did locate him in another city, where he was remarried and the father of two children. It wasn't easy to convince Mr. A about giving a *Get,* until we were able to help him understand that his second marriage had been entered into in violation of an orthodox religious ban.

In another case, that of the R family, it was only through the direct intervention by a rabbi in a southern city that we were able to help Mrs. R secure her *Get.* The couple had met in a concentration camp and there were two children. The marriage had never been a happy one and Mr. R left home several times. When he last deserted, we were asked to locate him. We did find him in a large city in the South. The local Jewish family agency found he had secured an uncontested divorce. Mrs. R was ready to accept it but wanted a *Get,* so that she would be free to remarry. Mr. R was reluctant to cooperate. We wrote to a Rabbi in the city who visited Mr. R and convinced him to grant the *Get.* When this was arranged Mrs. R agreed to the legal procedure for making the civil divorce effective.

There are often reverse situations in which we are called upon to interpret to a client that a *Get* which has been granted without a civil divorce is insufficient in civil law to entitle the parties to remarry.

Occasionally we may become involved in the search for the brother of a deceased husband of a childless widow in connection with *Chalitza.* In one particular case, which comes to mind at the moment, we did locate the unwed brother in another country only to be frustrated by the inability of our client to come face to face with the brother. These are, fortunately, rare exceptions.

Too often we are troubled by the dilemma of the *Agunah* who has succeeded in getting a dissolution of the civil marriage on the ground of unlocatable absence of the husband for over five years—very often after we in Family Location Service have made an exhaustive search and have testified as to the inability to locate. Yet the wife is not free to remarry under orthodox law because there has been no *Get*.[1]

Of more recent vintage are the cases we have of Israeli husbands here in the United States who have deserted their families in Israel; or of Americans who have married Israeli women and who have returned to the States; or of couples who have been divorced in Israel under religious law, with questions often involving the validity of such divorce in American courts.

In one case, the Israeli Consul asked us to locate a Benjamin D who had left his family in Israel back in 1950. Mrs. D wished to secure a *Get*. We learned that Mr. D was a collector for various Jewish institutions, visiting synagogues throughout the country. We alerted the rabbis of several eastern cities. One of these wrote us to say he had discussed the matter with Mr. D when he had arrived in his city and that he had convinced Mr. D to give a *Get*, which had since been forwarded to an Israeli rabbi for delivery to Mrs. D.

There are also cases in which we find that the marital difficulty results, in some measure, from differences as to the nature of Jewish commitments between the spouses and/or between the *mechotonim* (the families of the spouses).

For example, one of our cases involved an American rabbi whose wife had left him. He had married her, a Polish emigré, in Paris while he was on leave from his post as an army chap-

[1] See Zukerman, Jacob T., "Woman in Chains," *The Jewish Spectator,* Dec. 1951, pp. 24–26.

lain. She had come from a non-religious environment and she was never interested in her role as a *rebbitzin* and unsympathetic to his having to work evenings and weekends with Sunday School and other synagogal obligations. This led to quarrels which resulted in her leaving him. (Incidentally, this marriage has since been dissolved — legally and religiously.)

How the in-laws can add to the problems of a troubled marriage is illustrated by the W case in which Mr. W's parents refused to eat in the W household because they were not satisfied with the observing of *Kashruth* by their daughter-in-law. The W's had already been having difficulties because Mrs. W thought her husband was too dependent upon his parents for financial help. She felt that her in-laws were too domineering and she resented her mother-in-law's criticism of the way she ran a Jewish home. She brought to bear the influence of her own mother, who insisted that her daughter was just as correct in her observance of *Kashruth* as "that fancy *mechutenesteh* of mine."

In other cases, problems may have developed around the Jewish education of the children, whether they should be sent to a Yeshiva or not.

Take, for example, the disagreements in the T family. The couple were recent immigrants from Hungary. Mr. T was a devout member of a well-known Hassidic group. There were two children of this marriage. Mrs. T had a nine-year-old son by a previous marriage. She decided to send this boy to a modern Yeshiva which required her to remove the boy's *pais* before accepting the boy. She did this without consulting her husband. This led to a violent scene in which Mr. T. beat not only his step-son, but his wife as well. In the counseling sessions which ensued, it soon became clear that among the basic causes of the marital conflict were essential differences as to form of religious practices.

One man who had deserted his family was probably partly

goaded into disappearing by his wife's insistence on a particular type of bar mitzvah preparation. Mrs. R told us so herself. Her constant quarrels with Mr. R over money matters had been aggravated by her desire that their son Harvey attend a neighborhood Talmud Torah where most of Harvey's friends were students. Mr. R felt that it was a "waste of money to study for four years just to make a speech." He refused to pay the tuition, and left home. He was soon located and he agreed to return home and to accept referral to Jewish Family Service for counseling. In the meantime we arranged for a scholarship for the boy at the Talmud Torah. This made the preparation more acceptable to Mr. R. who in the process of counseling had agreed to recognize his wife's and his son's wish, even though he himself was not convinced of the need.

The matter of training becomes even more acute where the parents are either separated or divorced. Thus, after Mr. and Mrs. F had divorced, the wife was married again to a Mr. G, a very orthodox man. Mrs. G had custody of Joel, her son by the first marriage. She sent him to a Yeshiva. Mr. F objected, saying he was opposed to this and would not pay for it. He pointed out that the terms of the separation agreement gave him control of, as well as responsibility for, the boy's education. The mother pointed out that she was actually paying for the Yeshiva out of her present husband's earnings and was using the support money received from Mr. F only for other expenses. Yet the recriminations continue and the Court will be called upon to make a decision, if an agreement cannot be effected.

We have been active in a case in which the out-of-wedlock Catholic father of a child born to a Jewish woman had disappeared with the child, after having had the child baptized, without consent of the hospitalized Jewish mother. We located the father and learned that he had since married a Catholic and that they wished to bring up the girl in that faith. When the father realized that we planned to take court action, he agreed to return the child to the mother and to allow her to be brought up as a Jewess.

These are but a few examples of the many Jewish aspects of the problems that come to us and that are a very vital part of the cases in which Jewish families are involved.

In all of these we find that it is most helpful to the clients if our worker is attuned to the particularly Jewish components of the situation and if we are able to help the client to recognize the religious or cultural implications. Thus, for example, if a client is planning to divorce her husband, it may be important for her to understand that her religious remarriage may be impossible without the granting of a *Get* by her first husband; and that even though it may appear to the client to be unnecessary in terms of her own feelings or persuasion, the eventual effect upon the future of the children of a second marriage may be serious. We know of a case in which the daughter of a second marriage found that her orthodox prospective husband refused to marry her because the bride's mother had never received a *Get* from her first husband, and thus the daughter was not the child of a valid Jewish marriage.

As we try to help these clients, it is comforting to know that when religious problems arise we are able to call upon the facilities of the Commission on Synagogue Relations for interpretation and guidance to our workers as we attempt to be helpful to the families who come to us.

How can these families call upon us? We are available to any Jewish client in the greater New York area who has a problem arising out of the absence of a family member and/or in respect to failure to support. We see clients only by appointment, which may be made by telephone or by letter, and we have already worked out a special procedure with the Commission on Synagogue Relations whereby a rabbi may refer a situation by use of a specific referral form. It is helpful to receive from the rabbi something of the social background of the family and what he knows of the problem. For, in working together, we may be able to help the client arrive at a much better understanding of the basic problems which may have led to the family disruption. And very often the additional information made available to us by the rabbi may prove helpful in the development of our own worker's plan for seeking the missing person or working with the deserted family itself.

As is typical of all agencies in the Federation constellation, Family Location Service stands ready to work closely with all sectors of the Jewish community as we provide a casework-oriented location and legal aid service to the families who need our help. We like to feel that the Jewish client who comes to us may find additional comfort in knowing that there will be an appreciation of the Jewish aspects of any problem with which he may come — and certainly the "Yiddish hartz und neshomeh" (Jewish heart and soul) which has always been the symbol of Jewish brotherhood.

THE BLACK JEWISH COMMUNITY : PLIGHT, PROBLEM, PRIORITY
by
Rabbi Irving J. Block
The Brotherhood Synagogue

We have too long overlooked the problem at our own back door — "in the tents of Shem" there dwell thousands of black-skinned Jews, who affirm their faith in God, twice daily, by declaring the Shema. They are a part of us, spiritually tied to us, and yet they are estranged from us. Worse still, *we* are estranged from *them*.

I know that nearly all of us here have at some time met a Negro Jew. Some can relate that Negro Jewish children studied in their religious school and Talmud Torah. Others have had the honor of a black-skinned Israelite become a bar mitzvah in his synagogue. When I was in Albany recently, one of our colleagues recalled how a black Jew led the congregation in a prayer service, with beautiful diction and exacting "negun." The references are numerous. As individual rabbis, we have managed to cope with those Negro Jews who have knocked on our doors—but now the time has come to take concerted action.

There are thousands of such individual black-skinned Jews who form a sizeable community, to whose needs, plight, and problems we must give priority. The exact number remains to be ascertained, but this we do know—there are about twelve congregations in greater New York; their membership is comprised of men, women, young people, and children with fine, personable, and appealing qualities. I have come to know of their warmth and friendliness as well as their pride in and their love for Judaism. Their synagogue attendance, for *Shabas* and *yom tovim*, is strong and conscientious . . . their observance of *kashruth,* their faithful adherence to *bris milah, chupah kedushin* and many other essential practices is firm and meaningful.

The young people especially have become zealous for more religious education than their parents or mentors can impart. Yeshiva University has an Ethiopian Hebrew enrolled in its Teachers' Institute; Jewish Theological Seminary, in its Adult Education Program graduated a Negro Jewish young man, presumably highest in his class; Dropsie College has had several Negro Jews enrolled in its teachers' program and they, too, were highly esteemed because of their proficiency in their studies. In the more elementary programs, Negro boys and girls in New York have graduated from the Downtown Talmud Torah, Jacob Joseph, Bas Yaakov and similar schools.

Not many months ago, a group of young adults, aware of the challenging times in which we live, set about to organize and unify their *Kehillah*. In this regard it should come as no surprise to learn that they have their problems too, as we have had and still have ours in community coordination. The name which they chose for themselves was *Tsa-ah Harishon,* The First Step. Let me read a few succinct statements from the aims and objectives of this group :

1. To link ourselves with our brethren—in keeping with the principle כל ישראל חברים (all Israelites are brothers).

2. To assist our brethren to uphold Judaic practice and traditions and the study of Torah, in keeping with the principle, כל ישראל ערבים זה בזה (all Israelites are responsible for each other).

3. To train the young and talented people of the Ethiopian Hebrew Community to be leaders of our communities as rabbis, cantors and teachers—in keeping with the principle במקום שאין אנשים השתדל להיות איש (in the place where there is no man, strive thou to be their leader).

4. To draw inspiration and strength from our Black Jewish brethren, even as they may draw inspiration and encouragement from all Israel in keeping with the words of the Prophet Isaiah, איש את רעהו יעזרון (they helped every man his neighbor).

5. To encourage the full participation of the Black Jewish Community in the activities of the total American Jewish Community, in keeping with the principles of Hillel, אל תפרוש מן הצבור (Do not separate yourself from the community).

The hour of action has approached. We must train the young and capable men and women of the black Jewish community for positions of leadership in the community at large. We must select and encourage those who have an ardent desire to build the Kingdom of God, to study for the rabbinate and be ordained from our seminaries. Their talented vocalists must become *chazanim* and be numbered among the sweet singers of Israel; their fine and intelligent young people must be prepared as religious school teachers.

We must go even further. We must furnish scholarships for the countless Negro Jewish children whose parents cry out that their children are neglected and who, because of very modest incomes, cannot afford the cost of matriculation.

There are a host of matters and a multiplicity of problems which await our attention and the facilities of the Federation.

But this is not only a call for assistance. The fact is that we, the white-skinned Jewish community, desperately need to close ranks with the black-skinned Jewish community. In the great moral crises which confront our nation, I declare that a community of Negro Israelites, steeped in the traditions of our forefathers, immersed in the laws and ethics of our religious civilization — I declare that this group has the opportunity to make a worthwhile and lasting contribution to the entire Negro people of America. Who better than the Jew knows the sense of collective justice and community responsibility? Who better than the Negro Jew can reach his brother of like skin at a time of tension, mistrust, hostility, and growing anti-Semitism among the Negro people of America?

I beg of us to give this our first and foremost attention. Let our pulpits declare that the mandate of racial equality and religious brotherhood applies with equal emphasis, if not more, to our Negro Jewish brethren. Let us be mindful of the principle enunciated by the prophet Amos: "Are ye not as the children of the Ethiopians unto Me, O Children of Israel? saith the Lord."

REPORT OF THE COMMISSION ON SYNAGOGUE RELATIONS
by
Leonard Benari

An urgent and immediate problem faces our black Jewish brethren here and now. I will therefore write about it from their viewpoint — the viewpoint of the *Tsa-ah Harishon* (The First Step).

One important fact must be emphasized as basic to the nature of the black Jewish communities and to our understanding of them. They have, no less than all so-called people of color, been deprived of direct involvement in American society because of the dehumanizing process of segregation. Forced to live on the periphery of white society together with other non-whites, the black Jews, caught up in the Negro dilemma, have linked their aspirations with those of the Negro community.

If the rabbinic dictum *Al tifrosh min hatzibur* (do not separate yourself from the community) has been neglected in part by them, we are guilty of depriving them of the ability to fulfill this dictum. Since their aspirations for involvement in the mainstream of Jewish life have been thwarted by us, they have had to develop their own separate synagogues and schools. These separate synagogues and schools have not only become a source of pride and measure of self-respect, but have fulfilled a need to feel "at home" among their own kind, and have a sense of equality with *Klal Yisroel* in the sight of God. Here in a sense of being in "one's own home" they had the freedom to provide for their own social and cultural needs and to indulge in self-criticism as well as to castigate the oppressive white society.

This is the reason why many of our members in *Tsa-ah Harishon,* such as Joshua Hinkson, a graduate of Reb Jacob Joseph Yeshiva who is now a law school student, or Naomi

Franklin, who graduated from Beth Jaacob school in Williamsburg and attended two years of Yeshiva High School, were also active in congregations in the black Jewish community. Chaim Bibbins, whose two sons attend Yeshiva Zichron Moshe in the Bronx and who is a member of the Yeshiva's Men's Club, Mrs. Esther Bibbins, our chairman, whose three children attended the Downtown Talmud Torah and who is active with the PTA there, both affiliate with black Jewish groups as well.

Those of our membership who did attend such institutions of Jewish learning and who insist on their own children attending remark about the tragic hurt of racial prejudice they must undergo to study Torah.

That their own *schuls* become a refuge of social life for their members in the "Old World" Jewish sense is understandable. The "elder rabbi," who often does not have the Jewish educational background of his younger members, who attend Yeshivot and Talmud Torahs, enjoys much authority and prestige nevertheless. Without his guidance and peculiar intelligence in maintaining a balance between the two separate worlds, the religious and social structure of the black Jewish community could not exist.

The pride in their Jewish self-identification was expressed by a young lady who comes from a home where three generations of Black Jews live. She and I represented *Tsa-ah Harishon* at a Student Zionist sponsored forum at McGill University in Montreal last week.

"How far back do *you* go in your Jewish family identification?" she asked a student in the audience who questioned her right to be Jewish. "Do you have more certification than I have?"

One student with a beard and *payes* and wearing a *yarmulka* asked: "Do you put on *Tephilin*?"

"No!" she answered. "Only the males in our *schul* put on *Tephilin*."

"Do you *dovin* like we do?" he continued to ask.

"We *dovin* like orthodox Jews do," she retorted.

Such questions asked in all innocent curiosity, without malicious intent, anger those black Jews who take their devotion to the study of Torah and religious duty for granted, particularly when they come from non-observing Jews as they often do. This has been a major obstacle to various studies of the community attempted by white Jews. Many of the spurious visits of journalists or more serious attempts by white Jews are never directed to groups who are of prime importance. They just refuse to get involved. All studies thus far are of one particular group which invites such queries.

This is why *Tsa-ah Harishon* is attempting a self study for the enlightenment and mutual understanding between the black Jews and their white co-religionists.

Foremost, the younger generation has organized to realize the urgent need for the education in institutions of Jewish learning that their children are deprived of by living in Negro neighborhoods. This crying need, a compulsion, becomes the focal point of every meeting, no matter what is under discussion. A recent case is that of a young father, a strict, orthodox Jew, whose two sons were sent away from Yeshiva (Zichron Moshe) when he lost his job. To whom could he turn? The Farband was the only organization willing to accept these children until their father was able to pay for their tuition. This father, however, is not satisfied with the Farband schooling. He feels that his children are being deprived of the Yeshiva education he desires for them. This same young man told me of having to sit segregated in back of the *schul* when he regularly attended services in Louisiana while serving in the armed forces of our country.

To an extent, black Jewish members of *Tsa-ah Harishon*

have achieved a measure of direct involvement in Jewish activities. The Student Zionist Organization at its conference at Camp Hadar, in Connecticut, this past summer, passed a resolution to support the aspirations of the black Jews for full involvement in Jewish life. Our young people immediately joined the Student Zionist Organization and many joined particular Zionist organizations with enthusiasm.

Greater opportunity for more direct involvement in Jewish life is a matter of urgency with them. They are circumsized by the same ritual *Mohels* of our community as are their white co-religionists; they observe "ritual purification," *Kashruth* and the traditions as well as a religious devotion stemming from a profound love of God. Theirs is a true sense of religious duty. Why are they denied? At this most desperate and potentially critical time in America today, when we must find a dialogue between white and black to preserve our society, the black Jew can play a vital role. We Jews, in particular, in assessing our Jewish ethics and morals, have in the black Jew not only a source of mutual strength, but an instrument in fulfilling the role we continually play in building a better society through the instrument of Jewish ethics and morals. *Kol Yisroel arevin ze Lozeh* : "Everyone in Israel is responsible for one another." We must not be guilty of disregarding this *mitzvah* nor can we deprive those who devote themselves to *Torah L'shmah* from doing so.

THE MUTUAL RESPONSIBILITIES BETWEEN COMMUNAL SERVANTS AND THE COMMUNITY
by
Professor Moshe Zucker

What does Jewish tradition and law say concerning the mutual responsibilities that exist between the communal servant and the community? The formulation of the problem already assumes that these responsibilities involve, at least in some respects, legal and ethical principles different than those that govern relationships between usual employers and employees.

The basic difference between working for an individual and serving a community is expressed by Jewish tradition in one word. A business relationship between individual parties is termed as משא ומתן, giving and taking since the operating principle in such a relationship is actually one of give and take. Whereas service to the community is referred to as עמל or even עבדות, slavery, because this relationship is inspired by the idea of complete dedication and not by the mere principle of give and take. Of course in both cases, whether one works for an individual or for a community, the pivotal requirement is faithfulness and loyalty. There is, however, a fundamental difference between the loyalty one owes to an individual and that which one has to render to the community.

Faithfulness to the individual is determined by an agreement; faithfulness to the community corresponds to the ideals for which the community stands. Serving the community often requires immunization to one's own personal interests. Responsibility to an individual corresponds to values limited in scope and time. Service to the community brings one face to face with values which are as boundless in scope as they are limitless in time.

Judaism rejects all kinds of slavery. The only type of slavery sanctioned by Judaism is servitude to the community. And, it should be noted that not only those who serve the community on a purely idealistic basis enter the category of העוסקים בצרכי צבור thereby becoming a link in the endless chain of history, but also those who render their services to the community in return for payment. The author for this ruling is none other than the saint and scholar of our own time, the Chofetz, Chaim of the Yeshiva in Radim.

These ideological differences between private and public service are not without legal, practical consequences. A few examples will illustrate this point :

The Talmudic sage Rava (299–358) ruled that the teachers of the young, ritual slaughterers, healers, and city clerks who have been inefficient in their work may be discharged without prior warning. (Baba Bathra, 21B.) In this statement, as formulated in the Gemara, Rava does not explicitly limit his ruling to public workers only. But Maimonides, the foremost authority in Jewish law, interpreted Rava's dictum as referring only to those teachers, clerks, etc., who were engaged by the community. This interpretation was adopted by Rabbi Joseph Karo and codified in the *Shulchan Aruch* (see *Chosen Mishpat*, 336; 8, and Rambam, Shiroth, X, 7).

The study of Torah supersedes all other *mitzvot*, as articulated in Mishina's statement ותלמוד תורה כנגד כולם. The only action that is on par with Torah study is action on behalf of the community as expressed by the Palestinian sage, Ryemiah. העוסק בצרכי צבור כעוסק בדברי תורה (Yerushalmi, B'rachoth V, I). According to the Talmud, a person whose only and exclusive preoccupation is the study of Torah is not supposed to interrupt his studies in order to recite the *Shema* at its prescribed time. The same exemption is granted to those who are engaged in pressing communal work (Tosephta Brachoth I, 4; Rambam VI, 8). Public workers are therefore advised to schedule their prayers and religious activiites so that they would not conflict with their professional duties.

Jewish scholars of all ages have endeavored not to become involved in communal work lest the burden of such responsi-

bilities hinder them in their Torah study. Yet, in times of
emergency, when they were confronted with communal tasks
that could not be carried out by others, the תלמידי חכמים
were always ready to sacrifice their studies to the needs of
the community. One could cite many Talmudic passages in
corroboration of this fact, but I will confine myself to one
example taken from the Palestinian Talmud (Chagiga, 1, 7).
The sage Rabbi Abbauh lived, as is well known, in the city of
Caesarea, a city that was densely populated with people of
different guilds and different creeds. He was, therefore, deeply
engrossed in public affairs, especially in the struggle of defend-
ing Judaism against the allegations and accusations of the
Judeo-Christians who had their center in that city. His gifted
son, Chanina, was sent by his father to Tiberias to study at
the Academy headed by Rabbi Yochanan. After some time,
Rabbi Abbauh learned that his son Chanina engaged in communal welfare, to the neglect of his studies. The father then
sent to his son the following message : המבלי אין קברים בקסרין
שלחתיך לטבריא Had I wanted you to bury yourself in communal
work, I would not have sent you away from Caesarea. But
the other rabbis of Caesarea sharply disagreed with Rabbi
Abbauh. They contended that in times of need communal
welfare takes precedence, even to Torah. Very often we hear
the question of conflict in interest discussed. The demand to
avoid even a remote possibility of conflict in interest is presented in Talmudic literature in the following instance : "If
the collectors [of charity] still have money but no poor to
whom to distribute it, they should change the small coins into
larger ones, but not from their own money. If the stewards of
a charity kitchen [have food left over and] no poor to whom
to give it, they may sell it to others but not to themselves lest
they fall under suspicion of striking a bargain with goods
belonging to the poor."

Beyond the responsibilities of the communal worker to the community, what are the responsibilities of the community to its employees? To begin with one of the most important communal servants, the teacher : In our traditional literature it is generally accepted that teachers of religious subjects are not entitled to a full remuneration for their work. The salary they receive is considered merely as a reward for watching the children, as formulated in the Babylonian Talmud (Nedarim 37a) or as a compensation for not being able to engage in any other work, שכר בטלה as the formula goes in the Palestinian Talmud (Yersuhalmi, Nedarim IV, 3). Some rabbis who were asked to arbitrate disputes between teachers and the community rendered decisions in favor of the community under the assumption that a teacher's salary is only a compensation for time lost.

With due respect to the ingenuity of the Talmudic sages as well as to the erudition of the codifiers and later rabbis, we cannot help stating that this concept with regard to the salary paid to teachers of religion is based on a conjectural explanation of a Mishna and is not in accord with the primary sources.

The relevant Mishna (Nedarim IV, 3) states in effect : if A is *under vow* not to receive favors of monetary value from B, B is not permitted to teach A the Bible, but he is permitted to give him instruction in the oral law and lore — Midrash, Halachoth, and Agadoth. Also B is permitted to instruct the children of A even in the Bible. The sages of the Talmud endeavored to explain why the Mishna differentiated between teaching the person under vow the Bible and teaching him oral law.

The explanation suggested in the Gemara is that the instruction in the Bible has tangible monetary value since the Bible is usually taught to youngsters, and youngsters have to be watched by the teacher. A teacher of the Bible, therefore, may receive money in exchange for watching the children. It is also suggested that the teaching of Bible is accompanied by teaching of the thrope (cantation), for which one may receive payment, since this does not fall under the definition of Torah. The instruction of oral law and lore, on the other hand, which is usually imported to adults, who don't have to be watched, is to be given gratis and has, therefore, no monetary value.

In the further exposition of this Mishna, along the same lines. the Gemara encountered additional difficulties and even had to resort to textual criticism and declare the text of the Mishna defective (Nedarim 37a). However, it appears that all the difficulties in the understanding of this Mishna came as a result of the fact that the sages of the Gemara interpreted it in the light of conditions that prevailed in *their* time, instead of approaching it in the light of conditions in the time of the Mishna. In the period of the Amorahim, the interpreters of the Mishna, Jewish public schools were as a result of deteriorated general conditions already disorganized, so that the education of children was again in the hands of private tutors, whereas in earlier times, in the period of the Tanaim, the authors of the Mishna, education was the responsibility of the community, which supported free public schools. Seen in this light our Mishna becomes self-explanatory. A, who is under vow not to receive any favors of monetary value from B, may still be taught by B in the subject of oral law, which is of no monetary value because A can study it in the public school without paying any tuition. On the other hand, B is not allowed to teach A the Bible because A, as an adult, has no access to the elementary school, where the Bible is taught gratis, and therefore can study the Bible only with a private teacher whom he would have to pay. It now becomes quite clear why B is permitted to teach the children of A any subject: they as youngsters have access to all types of schools, so that the instruction they receive is in no case of monetary value to the father. Our premise with regard to the community obligations toward both the teachers of the Bible and teachers of the Mishna is clearly reflected in another source which reads: Said Rabbi Shimon Ben Yochai: "When you see communities in the land of Israel devastated you can be sure that these communities did not fulfill their duty in paying the salaries of the teachers in the Bible and instructors of the Mishna." (Yerush. Chagiga 1.) The notion that the salary of the מלמדים is merely a compensation and not a full-fledged payment for their skilled work, while a lofty idea, has no historic basis.

Like the payment to מלמדים, so the salary of judges and spiritual leaders, as well as aid for scholars not holding official positions in the community, became subjects of academic controversy. The most rigorous stand in this matter was taken by Maimonides. No student of the Torah, he contends, is permitted to use his knowledge for a source of income. Maimonides was well aware that here he was in disagreement with many other authorities, but he dismissed any opinion to the contrary as erroneous and biased. (See his commentary on Pirke Aboth IV, 5.) This opinion of Maimonides is forcefully contradicted by Rabbi Shimon Ben Tzemach Duran (Talmudist and philosopher of the 14–15th centuries). Not without sarcasm, Duran states that Maimonides was in a good position to preach such idealism and self-effacement because he had the good fortune to be both a physician and a friend of the king of Egypt. His income was pretty much secured (see Tashbatz 142–148).

An examination of the sources bearing on this problem, Talmudic and post-Talmudic, presents ample evidence that this controversy between Maimonides and Duran actually goes back to earlier times. Some scholars preferred to be supported by the people, or to receive a steady salary lest they be hampered in the pursuit of their Torah studies. The main proponent of this position, Rabbi Shimon Ben Yochai, reasoned: "If a person should plow, sow, harvest, thresh, and winnow in the appropriate seasons, what will become of his Torah. We therefore concluded that the scholar is entitled to have others take care of his personal needs. (B'rachoth 35b.) Others chose to combine some worldly occupation with their studies so that they might enjoy a full degree of freedom and independence in rendering their decisions to the community. Scholars of the first type, like Rabbi Shimon Ben Yochai and his associates, were designated as ת"ח שתורתן אומנותן scholars, whose profession is Torah. The other type of scholars, like the famous Amora K. Yochanan, the Rosh Yeshiva of Tiberias, were referred to as ת"ח שאין תורתן אומנותן scholars for whom Torah is not a means of livelihood. (שבת י"א, א: ברכות י"ז, א) There is no doubt about it that the greater majority of judges and ראשי ישיבות in talmudic times did receive a steady salary from their respective communities.

The exilarchs, the worldly leaders of Jewry, in Babylon, in the early Medieval times, even developed a special taste for abundance and affluence. They employed all possible and impossible means, persuasive and coercive, in collecting donations and taxes from the community under their jurisdiction. The ראשי ישיבות of that same period, the Gaonim who presided over the *Yeshivoth*, likewise taxed the people in order to secure comfortable maintenance for themselves and their disciples. The tactics applied by some of the exilarchs and Gaonim in this respect evoked protests and dissatisfaction on the part of the people.

It is quite plausible that the malcontent of the communities burdened with such taxation contributed toward the rise of the *Karaite* sect, which probably was not only a religious movement but also a kind of social revolution against the leaders of that time. Leading Karaites frequently lashed out at the exilarchs and ראשי ישיבות, criticizing their behavior in this respect.

Still later, in the Spanish and Franco-German period, as well as in the Eastern European communities, rabbis ראשי ישיבות and preachers (*magidim*), with very few known exceptions, drew a steady salary from their community. Some of them were modest and pious enough to content themselves with a minimum. Such self-effacement of a rabbi is portrayed by the contemporary Hebrew author, Chaim Hazaz. He describes a rabbi of unusual keenness and ingenuity who had an answer for every question against the Gemara or the Rambam but was helpless to answer the question raised by his poor wife and children: "What should we eat?" When the head of the Kahal one day suggested a modest increase in salary to this rabbi, he replied: "I don't need it. צרכי כפי מה שיש לי ויש לי כפי צרכי My needs are in accord to what I have, and what I have is in accord with my needs." Others, on the contrary, knew how to exploit their rights and privileges to a fuller extent. All in all, throughout history, the idea of serving the community in the capacity of teacher, rabbis or ראשי ישיבות without payment proved to be rather Utopian.

This conclusion leads us to another problem: to what extent are communal servants (such as rabbis, teachers, doctors, social workers, etc.) entitled to protect their material interests by the employment of coercive means (including unionization, strikes, etc.)? This problem is of special relevance as the question of organized labor by communal servants has been raised frequently here in our own country and abroad, and is especially timely in our beloved land of Israel, where strikes seem to be regularly alternated with work.

In seeking a solution to this problem we must first elucidate a question of a more general nature, namely, is there in Talmudic-rabbinic literature any basis for the modern labor concepts of unions, closed shops, collective bargaining, and strikes? The idea of mutual protection by workers, as well as trade unions and guilds, is alluded to in Talmudic sources. In the Tosephtah Baba Mez. 11, 25) we read : רשאין הנחתומין לעשות רגיעה ביניהם bakers are permitted to agree amongst themselves on a *Regiah*. The somewhat enigmatic term *Regiah* was taken by medieval scholars as a derivative of the Hebrew verb רגע which means rest. They, consequently, explained the sentence to the effect that the bakers are entitled to make an agreement whereby they will alternate days of work, so that one would rest while the others work. So understood, such an agreement aimed at avoiding over-production, which would lead to spoilage of merchandise and a fall in prices. (Actually we find in another Talmudic source such an agreement between two ritual slaughterers : Baba Bathra 9ª.) Modern scholars disagree with this interpretation of the term *Regiah*. They correctly recognize in the term *Regiah* a parallel to its Arabic cognate *Ragatun* which denotes mutual agreement. The nature of the agreement is thus not spelled out in the *Tosephta*. However one may assume with a high degree of certainty that such agreements were in the nature of mutual aid as well as safeguarding against competition by newcomers. Similar agreements are alluded to in the same *Tosephta* and in other sources. Of special interest, historically, is the agreement among coachmen to replace the fallen horse of a bereaved owner with another at the expense of the guild. Such mutual agreements were in a later period declared valid only with the provision that the local legal authority give his consent to it (Baba Bathra 9ª).

The right of collective bargaining is simply assured in Talmudic law since everybody is entitled to appoint an agent to act on his behalf.

More complicated is the problem of strikes in Jewish law. Can we find a basis for it in Talmudic or post-Talmudic literature? Some scholars have based the right to strike on the well-known Talmudic dictum (Baba Metziah 77ª) פועל יכול

לחזור בו אפילו באמצע היום a worker is entitled to
interrupt his work and release himself from a contract at any
time of the day. On more careful observation, however, it
becomes clear that this ruling has no relevance whatsoever
to the right of strike, for more than one reason.

1. The majority of scholars are of the opinion that a worker may
   release himself from the agreement only in cases where he has
   decided to give up this kind of work altogether. He is not, on
   the other hand, entitled to break his agreement in order to
   assume the same kind of work in another place under more
   favorable conditions.

2. The right of the worker to leave his work in the midst of his
   contract is also restricted to cases in which only a verbal agreement between the employer and employee exists. In cases
   where a contract was put into writing, or was confirmed by
   other legally binding means (like the well-known (קבלת קנין)
   the worker is not entitled to break the contract.

3. Finally, and this is the most telling point, a strike as understood today is not merely a severence of ties with the employer,
   rather it is a way of compelling the employer to maintain the
   relation under changed conditions.

In 1944 the organization **Poel Hamizrachi** in Israel turned
to one of the leading rabbis there with the question that now
occupies our minds: Is striking permissible by the standards
of Jewish tradition? (See Zitz Elieser II, 23.) The learned rabbi
answered in the affirmative and based his decision mainly on
the following sources:

1. In the first Mishna of chapter 7 in the Tractat Baba Metzia
   we read: "If a man hired workers and told them to come to
   work early before dawn and leave the work after dark he is

not allowed by law to compel them to do so if it is contrary to the custom prevailing in that place."

2. There is a paragraph in the Tractat of Baba Bathra (8b) to the effect that the people of the city—or their representatives —are entitled to fix prices, measures, and wages and also to impose sanctions upon disobedient individuals (see also Tosephta Baba Metziah XI, 23).

3. There are many Responsa of medieval scholars in which the authority of the representatives of the community over its members is strongly defended.

Combining these three sources, this rabbi arrives at the following conclusions:

1. The representatives of the community possess the authority to control labor-management relations with regard to daily hours of work, as well as in regard to wages.

2. These representatives are entitled to employ sanctions against individuals who refuse to act in accordance with their decisions.

3. These representatives consequently possess the authority to sanction strikes as a means of coercing the employer to live up to the standards which have been set.

With all due respect to the very learned rabbi I am not in a position to agree with his interpretation of the sources. The Mishna in Baba Metzia that he quoted does not refer to a case where the employer and employees entered into an explicit agreement contrary to local practices, as is partially admitted by himself at the beginning of the Responsum. On the contrary, if such an agreement had taken place at the time of the hiring, its validity would not have been challenged in spite of its being at variance with local custom. This is the opinion of the commentators, the so-called Todafists, and so it has been codified in Shulchan Arukh (Choshen Mishpot, 331, 1). It is also reflected in the remarks of the Gemara on that Mishna. The Mishna simply says that if the employer hired the worker without specifying his terms we may assume that the workers took it for granted that the local prevailing customs would determine their conditions too. It is considered a kind of a tacit agreement. There is thus no allusion, whatsoever, to the idea that an explicit agreement becomes invalidated if it is in discord with local practice. The paragraph he quoted from the Tractat of Baba Bathra in regard to the authority of the representatives of the community over prices and wages is in no way to be construed as authorizing the community's representatives to compel an employer to raise the wages of his employees. Rather it means that the community may reduce prices and wages in order to protect itself against the menace of inflation.

This correct interpretation of the passage is given by one of the greatest Talmudic authorities, who is also famous as a leader of the European communities of his time: Rabenu Gershom Meor Hagolah — *The Luminary of the Exile*. The Responsa quoted by Rabbi Waldenberg merely empowered the representatives of the community to take remedial measures when the welfare of the entire community as such is at stake or when the Torah is infringed upon. In no way do the responsa authorize the community to enact legislation to the advantage of one of the parties and to the disadvantage of the other.

We thus, alas, have no basis in Talmudic-Rabbinic literature for the right to strike.

In absence of Jewish legislation concerning the strike, pro-or-con, we have no recourse but to employ the law of the land.

A well-known ruling of Mar Shmuel (Amora of the third century) states: **דינא דמלכותא דינא** the law of the land is binding in cases brought before a rabbinic court as long as it does not contradict an explicit law of the Torah or the Talmud. This ruling, in the predominant opinion of scholars, is applicable not only to laws pertaining to such interests of the government proper, as taxes, military services, etc., but also to civil laws, including, of course, labor-management relations. Consequently from the Talmudic point of view, we would sanction strikes in cases when they are legal according to the law of the land and would reject them in cases when they are declared illegal by the law of the country. This leads us directly to the solution of the problem regarding strikes by public employees. As long as federal and state laws declare such strikes inconsistent with the responsibilities of the public employees to the community, we may not sanction them from the Talmudic standpoint either.

In fairness to the public employee, some remarks should be added: From the standpoint of justice and equity we are perhaps bound to consider the disparity between the rights of public and private employees as contradictory to the Biblical maxim: **משפט אחד יהיה לכם** You shall have one standard of law. Any discrimination between the rights of one class of workers and those of another may even signify that the law of labor relations for public servants is inequitable and not completely developed. Moreover, one may argue that by depriving the public worker of the right to strike, the federal and state governments refuse to accept upon themselves legal standards which they established for others. Notwithstanding all these seeming inequities we must, from a purely Talmud-legalistic point of view, insist upon denying the right to strike to community employees as long as this right is not granted to them by the **דינא דמלכותא** — by the law of the land. Should the government change its attitude toward the problem, then we, from the point of view of Jewish tradition, would unhesitatingly follow suit, with one strong reservation : Jewish law would never grant the right to strike to people upon whom the safety of human life depends, like doctors and nurses. Our religion places the value of human life above all other values, so long as no denial of God's sovereignty is involved. The doctor, according to the teachings of Torah and Talmud, is responsible to the patient not because of his professional standards but because of his standards as a human being. One may, perhaps, under certain circumstances extricate himself from his duties as a possessor of a diploma but there is no escape from one's duties as a bearer of God's image.

The argument that even in cases of strike, hospital patients are not left without doctors in attendance is not sound. For, according to Jewish law, if a patient requests the care of a certain doctor, that doctor is not permitted to refuse his services even if there is another doctor available (תורת האדם לרמב"ן יורה דעה 336). It also may be mentioned in this context that according to Jewish law, when a seriously ill person requires on the Sabbath the services of a doctor who is a strict שומר שבת Sabbath observer, this doctor must follow the call of the patient and is not permitted to let himself be replaced by a Gentile or by a non-observant Jew.

These rulings are issued on the basis of a very fine observation made by a scholar of the Palestinian Talmud. (Nedarim IV, 2.) לא מכל אדם זוכה להתרפות The effectiveness of a doctor depends not only upon his skill and experience but also to a great extent upon the degree of trust and confidence the patient puts in him.

Our sages have coined a wonderful phrase : לפום צערא אגרא — One's reward is proportionate to the responsibilities he assumes, to the efforts he makes, and to the pain and strain he endures. The responsibilities of public servants are, as we have seen, greater than those of other workers. Their rights and privileges should be guarded and protected accordingly. The welfare of the public servant determines the welfare of the public itself. A malcontent servant is an inefficient servant.

Teaching, curing, patching broken families, and similar tasks are creative work, and their success is always related to the mood of the worker. Our conclusion, therefore, must be : The responsibilities of the community to its servants are as sacred and as great as are the responsibilities of the servants to the community.

2

Judaism and Social Welfare

The Religious Director of Federation recounts the signal achievement of the Commission on Synagogue Relations on its bar mitzvah anniversary, in nurturing the fruitful dialogue between rabbis, social workers, psychiatrists, and psychologists that has encompassed the entire range of problems in Jewish social welfare and their concern for the well-being of the individual Jew in our alienated society.

The philosophy of the Commission is that the 116 social health and welfare agencies of the Federation complex, individually and collectively, are committed to Jewish values and Jewish survival, even as they keep their doors open to non-Jews who seek their services.

This theme is reiterated in the varied areas of foster care, the residential treatment of disturbed children and their religious observance and education, and the relationships of adult children to aged parents.

Social welfare Judaism, as these papers reveal, is devoted to

75

the moral and religious ideal of the inviolability of the human spirit and the sanctity of life and personality — to do all it can to repair it where damaged, to try to restitch it where torn, and to preserve its health and prevent its disintegration whenever possible.

Thus, Elizabeth Radinsky asserts that the foster home under expert agency guidance can result in an enriched Jewish religious and educational development instead of its diminution. She emphasizes the fact that this also is psychologically beneficial to the foster child who needs a sense of community identity and belongingness.

"The Importance of Religion in the Residential Treatment of Disturbed Children," by Dr. Hector Ritey, is an absorbing, brilliant presentation of the impressive evidence why Jewish religious education is a sine-qua-non stability bulwark in working with and helping emotionally disturbed Jewish children.

Jack Adler makes incisive comments upon and additions to Dr. Ritey's paper, aided by apt examples of actual cases and situations. Mr. Adler emphasizes the fact that most Jewish children at the residential treatment centers have not experienced either a strong religious element or maturity in their parents. He asserts that religion and tradition are positive forces that reinforce a child's trust in life and the world about him, and therefore the Jewish component is a vital factor in the work of the residential treatment institution.

Rabbi Jack Bemporad continues the outstanding symposium with further comments on Dr. Ritey's presentation. Rabbi Bemporad takes the problem of the role of religion in respect to the children and their families one step further as it applies to the staff at the institution. He discusses the need of the religious program to develop a pattern of life on the part of the children that has continuity and reinforcement by the environment and the professional staff.

Completing the symposium, Paul Steinfeld stresses the use

of religious education to further the emotional development of a child who has alienated himself from his group and from his society. He states the necessity of making religious values a part of the institution's value system. Also, he says that the staff "must convey qualities of understanding, patience, forgiveness, justice, and other standards of human behavior and orderly existence" in their relationships with the children.

Gerald Beallor sets forth the moral ethical problems related to the mutual responsibilities of adult children and aged parents. Mr. Beallor's case studies illustrate the problems of aged parents and how Jewish Family Service provides help to carry them through a critical period.

The Jewish community lost an incisively perceptive, able, and dedicated civil servant with the untimely passing of the late William Posner. Typical of his Jewish commitment and the solid rationale on which it was founded is his firm presentation of the significantly positive role which Jewish content and climate play in the help our social-work agencies give.

THE RABBI, THE JEWISH SOCIAL WORKER AND A BAR MITZVAH
by
Rabbi Isaac N. Trainin

It is now thirteen years since Federation commenced its pioneering work on the relationship between the rabbinate and the Jewish social work profession in the New York area. For our purposes, we shall define Jewish social work broadly to include the case worker, the group worker, the psychiatrist, the sociologist, and the psychologist. On this bar mitzvah occasion, it is most appropriate to review the history of this relationship and to make some personal observations and comments.

The challenge that faced us was monumental. We were

dealing with a community of a thousand synagogues and as many rabbis; we were dealing with a multiplicity of Jewish welfare agencies—the largest anywhere in the world. I vividly recall the first attempts made by Federation's Religious Affairs Department in convening a group of rabbis and social workers early in December, 1952. I recall the hostility of colleagues in the rabbinate and the skepticism of some of my colleagues in the social work profession. It seemed at that time that the distance between the two disciplines would be difficult to bridge. Each discipline seemed to be perched on its own mountain top. Separating them was a valley of indifference. Looking back over the past thirteen years, it is apparent that miracles are achievable, but that they are not recognizable for a long time. In the spirit of Chanukah על הנסים ועל הפרקן we can give thanks for the miracles that have been wrought.

During this period, we have witnessed the flowering of a new era. Rabbis, social workers, psychiatrists, and psychologists have met on a continuous basis to think together, to reason together, and to find ways of mutual cooperation. By now our work has been emulated in many communities and hopefully many others will undertake this experiment.

In this interval, we have involved the rabbi and the Jewish social worker in dialogues and confrontations covering an enormous range of topics. Commencing with the Committee on the Relationship of the Rabbi to the Jewish Social Worker, we have broadened and continued to broaden our base. We have conducted tours for rabbis at Federation agencies, where they learned at first hand the functions of their services. Some of our agencies have conducted workshops for rabbis, in which rabbis and social workers reviewed cases which would delineate the areas of cooperation between the two. Workshops have been held on Mental Health and Judaism, the Jewish Component in the Treatment of Emotionally Disturbed Children; the roles of the YMHA and the synagogue in formal and informal Jewish education; how the synagogue and our agencies can cooperate in integrating the black Jews into the overall community; how the rabbi and the social worker can cooperate in problems of divorce and separation. The synagogue and our family agencies have pioneered in bringing order out of chaos in the area of the transients and the indigents. A number of agencies have invited rabbis to join their Boards and have involved local rabbis in many consultative capacities. Through our Speakers Bureau, a number of leading social workers have been invited to speak before synagogue groups. One of our latest ventures is a program involving our child care agencies and synagogues in an after-care program, whereby youngsters leaving Hawthorne and Pleasantville in particular will be integrated into the local community via a synagogue program. In cooperation with a number of "Y's," our young synagogue leadership is engaged in a pre-college orientation series. At these meetings these young men meet with high school juniors and seniors to orient them to what it means to live as a Jew on a college campus — especially in out-of-town universities.

The Rabbi and the Jewish Social Worker, the first in a series of books, has been published by our Commission. I suppose that one of our most significant achievements was the Conference on Intermarriage held in December, 1964, at which some of our most distinguished rabbinical colleagues and social workers came together to think through this grave threat to Jewish survival. Printed proceedings of the conference have met with widespread acceptance in the American Jewish community. We are continuing to work in this area with the full support of many rabbis and many social work colleagues. Our Jewish Family agencies, as a result of our recommendations, have appointed a liaison person for the New York rabbinate. This person will be available to the rabbi to discuss any counseling problem involving intermarriage. A number of outstanding papers especially prepared for the Commission, on topics of mutual concern to Judaism and Jewish social work, covering problems of the aged, mental health, child care, adoption, Tzedakah, etc., have resulted from our work. Our Hospital Compendium, the first in Jewish history, has now gone through two editions and has been purchased by hospitals and medical centers in every state of the Union and in over eighteen foreign countries.

During this period the Jewish Education Committee launched its Jewish orientation and training seminars which have helped social workers understand the Jewish community and which have given them a better understanding of Jewish tradition, customs, and law.

This unusual relationship developed slowly in an atmosphere of mutual understanding and trust. We have involved in our deliberations rabbis of all ideologies, synagogue lay leaders, and both lay and professional leaders in the social work profession. This has been a continuous conference of Jews, Jews, and Jews. We are proud of our success and rarely speak of our failures. These failures, if one wants to call them so, are basically due to the fact that we are not a monolithic community. Let us pause to recognize that there are four distinct Jews with whom we must deal. First, there is the secular assimilationist: Jewish by birth, he is not concerned about survival and the threat of assimilation; yet, from this rank come some of the most generous contributors to Jewish communal causes and the community's most ardent workers. Second, there is the secular survivalist: he represents a significant number of our people who are totally unconcerned with Judaism as a religion, but who are passionate in their determination that the Jewish people survive. Third, is the synagogue-affiliated Jew, who belongs because of a sense of conformity, but who would be hard put to define what Judaism means to him. Fourth, is the synagogue-affiliated survivalist, who is committed to the Jewish religion and to Jewish peoplehood and he is concerned about transmitting those values to his children. These then represent the people with whom we must work and surely the rabbi who, by and large, deals with a homogeneous group must understand this and sympathize with the social worker, whose function it is to create a rapport with every Jew, no matter what label he carries. Let us recognize that Judaism rarely presented a monolithic structure, that the schools of Hillel and Shmai, that the period immediately after the death of Maimonides, and that the struggle between the Hassidim and the Misnogdim represented Judaism in a state of flux and growth.

In an age of bigness, we are faced with what Justice Brandeis characterized as the curse of bigness. The individual has become a social security number, or a digit. We speak of factory hands, not people. We speak of hospital beds, not patients. The important synagogue is the one that boasts of a large membership and is housed in a multi-million-dollar structure. A social work agency is important if it can boast of tremendous waiting lists. In short, we talk of sizes and numbers. In this there is a danger for all of us of loving humanity but ignoring people. Jewish tradition teaches us that he who saves one life is as if he would save the whole world.

This, in essence, is, or should be, the philosophy of Jewish social work and the synagogue. We must be concerned for the individual. The Bible does not speak of loving one's neighbors, it says ואהבת לרעך כמוך and thou shall love thy neighbor. And furthermore, in the same chapter קדשים it states וכי יגור אתך גר בארצכם and if a stranger sojourns with thee in your land, Ye shall not do him wrong. Again the Bible speaks in the singular.

I am unhappy with the word *case* as used in the social work profession. We should be concerned about people, not *cases*. The nomenclature we use very often reflects our attitudes towards people and problems. Our rabbis should be concerned about individuals and not about a thousand members which their congregations may have. While studies and statistics are important, we should be concerned primarily about the individual. It is true that in Judaism the community is supreme; we pray together and we even repent for our sins in the plural. But, again, I repeat, our concern for the individual is what counts.

Let us be proud to be different. I recall a meeting with the Satmar Rabbi. He pointed out that beginning with the Pilgrims, the early colonists came to these shores in order to preserve these differences. It seems that the authors of the book *Beyond the Melting Pot* have proven to us how concerned ethnic groups are in preserving their own unique civilization.

I wonder if the sudden interest in Judaism and Jewish values cannot be due to the American intellectual's boredom with the grinding conformity and malaise corroding American civilization; and that he finds something refreshing and different in Jewish tradition and in the Jewish way of life. I wonder what significance there lies in the fact that so many of our people have become enamored of the "Fiddler on the Roof" and find a sense of nostalgia in the traditions that the play represents, which they, the viewers, have rejected in their own personal life.

Both the rabbi and the Jewish social worker must work together to help the Jew in our alienated society, for many Jews are doubly alienated—alienated as Americans and alienated from their Jewish roots. We must consider the Hebraic concept of לפנים משורת הדין and not be ossified in our own concepts which sometimes become like the laws of the Medes and Persians. Too often we are unable to help an individual because we accentuate the rule and ignore the exception. Let us strive to accentuate the exception and overlook the rule some time.

The rabbi cannot ask for the imposition of standards on Jewish agencies that he is not willing or unable to impose on his synagogue. The rabbi who has mixed dancing for his teenagers at the synagogue can hardly complain about the community center which follows the same policy.

By the same token, the social work profession must review its non-judgmental attitude, particularly in the area of inter-marriage. The Jewish social worker must have a commitment to Jewish values. When we are faced with a growing attenuation in our ranks, he must stand up and be counted together with the rabbi and others in our community who wish to preserve the Jewish community. The image which our synagogues and Jewish communal institutions create are most important for the kind of a Jewish community we will build.

The rabbi and the Jewish social worker who very often work with the same person must strive to present a unified front and not leave the client with the impression that what is important to the rabbi is irrelevant to the social worker and vice versa. Too often the policies of communal institutions reflect the biases and prejudices of individual members of their boards and staff rather than the needs of the Jewish community. If there are a lack of values in our Jewish community, should not our social work profession attempt to set up standards rather than reflect the lack of values?

The basic respect between the two disciplines cannot be overstated. Let the social worker look for ways to cooperate with the rabbi in every way possible. Let the rabbi spend less time criticizing the social work profession and instead recognize the fine work and dedication of many unsung heroes, who work and labor in behalf of the individual Jew in need of help.

Something about the relationship of the synagogue to the YMHA must be said. On the one hand, many rabbis criticize the "Y's" for lack of Jewish content; on the other hand, they are often disturbed when a particular "Y" introduces formal or informal Jewish education in its program. There are exceptional cases where conflict can arise, but generally speaking the religious community ought to encourage every "Y" to foster Jewish education. I am reminded of the complaint which Joshua made to Moses that a band of Jews were prophesizing. Moses's reply was significant: "Oh that all Jews were prophets." Oh that every YMHA were fully immersed in Jewish education and that every Jewish child would receive a Jewish education. We on the Commission, recognizing the contemporary situation, have accepted the fact that Sabbath programs, in consonance with the Sabbath, can be conducted by the "Y's." The problem is the interpretation of what is in consonance with the Sabbath. What disturbs the rabbi is that too often "Y's" become Halachic authorities and we suddenly find that programs are organized which would disturb all religious leadership, be it Conservative, Orthodox, or Reform ideologies.

Those of us who work with youth face almost insurmountable problems. They have not rejected Judaism, they have become indifferent to it. It has ceased to speak to and meet their innermost questions. They find challenge in Western thought and American culture. Jewish education has failed to achieve what is, or what is to be, its major purpose. Jewish education should help us to see our descent from Sinai as a contemporary event. It should heighten our sense of kinship and our affinity of spirit with Abraham and Jacob, with Yehudi Halevi and Maimonides, with the Bal Shem Tov, and Theodor Herzl. And this is true whether we deal with youth in the synagogue, the YMHA, in a camp, etc.

I have followed with great disquietude the practice of many rabbis and outstanding social scientists in quoting non-Jewish sources in their papers and speeches. Freud, Jung, Dewey, Adler, and others are often cited to prove, I suspect, that we are at home in Western culture. This is fine. I, on the contrary, would urge and plead with my colleagues in these two disciplines to dig into the well of our own heritage more often. It seems that so few of us realize what rich nuggets we will find there and how they touch on contemporary human problems.

It pleased me again and again when some of our social work colleagues requested that our conferences deal with the question: what does Jewish tradition have to say on various contemporary problems? How can we begin to impress the Jewish youth of today that our heritage and culture are worth preserving; that it speaks to the contemporary heart and mind — when we ourselves so often utilize strange gardens of knowledge and ignore our own backyard of wisdom?

Most important, we must resolve the ambivalence which exists today in our social work profession. Perhaps this can be best spelled out by Rabbi Hillel's famous injunction אם אין אני לי מי לי, וכשאני לעצמי מה אני׃ There are those who say "If I am not for myself, who will be," that institutions under Jewish auspices must serve only Jews. There are those who say, "If I am only for myself, what am I?" Those people profess the non-sectarian policy. The danger there is that we may become engulfed in the unfathomable abyss of secularism, wherein the Jewish nature of our programs will suffer irretrievably. The question we must ask ourselves, with Rabbi Hillel, is, "If not now, when?" The ambivalence must be resolved. I submit that the answer must lie in a philosophy which says: "We are a Jewish agency committed to Jewish values and Jewish survival. Wherever possible, we will not close our doors to non-Jews who seek our services, but this service must neither negate nor dilute our primary responsibilities." The danger of a minority culture becoming engulfed is precisely what the Bible had in mind when it spoke about "the statues of the Gentiles." It is a tragic fact of our existence as Jews that a great religion, the prophetic faith and culture of our people, the cornerstone of morality and religion in the Western world, has often been reduced to a technique of minority adjustment, an antidote to an inferiority complex. We must cease being frantically preoccupied with our survival as Jews and become wisely and deeply concerned with our total lives as Jewish persons. Many things separate us, but we have one thing in common. We may differ on what we mean by such words as Jewish people, or God, or revelation. We have one word in common—our least common denominator. It is the most important fact for each of us and all of us together. The word is the name *Jew*. The wisdom of the Bible recognized this early when in the second book it states ואלה שמות בני ישראל "And these are the names of the Children of Israel." Commentaries asked why the Bible, which is so concerned with economy of language, must repeat the names of Jacob's sons after they were enumerated in the preceding chapter. I would like to suggest a modern interpretation as to why the names were repeated. We know that even in Egypt, 4,000 years ago, there were Zionists, Nationalists, pro-Egyptians, and other types of Jews. That is why each tribe had to be enumerated separately. But they had one thing in common—they were all the children of Israel.

Let us all recognize that we must stand together behind the banner of Tzedakah, the great symbol, the glory, the power, and the essence of much of Judaic civilization. The price of divisiveness can only lead to agencies under ideological auspices. Let the word *Jewish* bind us and not separate us. The Jews, Moses complained, are a stiff-necked people, but I am reminded of the old song

וואָס מיר זיינען זיינען מיר, אָבער אידן זיינען מיר

what we are, we are, but Jews we are.

Many centuries and millennia separate us from our Father Abraham. By our concept of Tzedakah and concern for our fellow human being, we are his spiritual heirs. Let us always remember that Abraham was concerned for the stranger regardless of who he was.

Abraham was told to leave his land and לֶךְ לְךָ מֵאַרְצֶךָ his father's home and to wander into a strange land. We rabbis and social workers must reexamine some of our shopworn ideas and pet theories that we have about ourselves and about each other. We must go out and try to reestablish and rekindle our kinship to Father Abraham. In 1956, I said the following:

To those skeptics in both professions—and I know some—who feel that the irresistible force of the rabbinate, and the immovable fortress of the social worker cannot meet, my answer is simple: we in New York have made test studies with extraordinary results; let rabbis and social workers in every community give it a chance! If you will plant with patience, you will reap rich rewards in the vineyard of human relations.

It is my passionate belief that both professions are engaged in communal work which in our times is as necessary for the mental health of our community as medicine is for the physical well-being of humanity. Social work in its broadest implications is that phase of communal work extolled on each Sabbath in this prayer:

"And all those who are engaged in communal work with sincerity may the Lord give them their due reward." When Abraham and his son Isaac went up to Mt. Moriah, the Bible states: "And they both went together." The rabbi and the Jewish social worker are both climbing the Mr. Moriah of service to their people. Surely they must tread the path together.

I believe in our joint mission with all the fervor and passion at my command. Moses stood on Mt. Nebo in the Land of Moab and looked into the promised land which he would never enter. We, today, stand on the mountain facing an uncertain future for American Judaism.

To me the task is clear, the objectives are lofty and eternal. The time? — Rabbi Hillel put it best. ואם לא עכשיו אימתי If not now, when?

THE JEWISH COMPONENT IN FOSTER CARE

by

Elizabeth K. Radinsky

As a foster care agency for Jewish children, we have long since established a policy on Jewish Education,[1] recognizing the need for attention to the religious and cultural components in its child rearing responsibilities. As I look back it is clear that in spite of many problems — some of which are related to staff orientation — there has been by and large awareness and acceptance of responsibility for implementation of this policy for Jewish Education. The $23,292 spent in last year's budget is one bit of testimony.

As reported here, our experience in the foster home division relates to special aspects and complications. The children referred to are those in whose disturbance the factor of separation is markedly significant.

Many children in foster care, even some who come to us as infants, have already experienced disturbed and chaotic family settings that failed them, and have already planted seeds of distrust and insecurity. This is often the reason for placing them in foster homes — with the hope of correcting or offsetting the disruption of normal growth and personality development. However, our long experience with children in foster home placement has made it plain that as indicated by Dr. Ner Litt-

[1] *The Jewish Social Service Quarterly;* June 1946, Vol. XII, Number 4
"Jewish Education in a Foster Home Agency": William Posner
"Jewish Education in a Foster Home Agency—a Follow-up Report": Elizabeth K. Radinsky & Golde Bodek
Cultural Factors in Jewish Social Service—"Jewish Content in Child Placement": William Posner.

ner,[2] "later good experiences do not destroy the effect of earlier poor ones." A child's good relationship with his foster family cannot cancel out the earlier "impact of bad relationships." Foster family care can provide an alternate living experience that may "wall off and encapsulate the traumatic effects of the earlier one."[3]

Obviously, a foster home, different as it may be from the child's own family setting, creates for the child and his family —and most of our children have families—a very different constellation of factors from the institutional setting. These factors demand attention and scrutiny in the implementation of the agency's responsibility for the religious and Jewish educational development of the child. Theoretically we place a child in a foster home in keeping with his Jewish background. In practice, this means that for the orthodox child we make every effort to find the appropriate home for him in terms of religious observances, sometimes even with some compromise in regard to his total needs. As to the other children—the majority of our population—of whom the larger number come from families as described by Mr. Adler, where this is little more than "nomenclature" identification with Judaism, these children are placed with qualifying foster families selected primarily with a consideration to the child's total needs and his family situation. Here there is no particular concern with the denomination of Judaism practiced—as long as there is acceptable identification and practice. We are mindful always that a fundamental asset of foster family care is its potential for providing the child with ego-ideals, mature persons with whom to identify. However, in the process of developing identification with the foster parents the realization of his own parents' inadequacies may be sharpened—or conflicts with values may be created—or there may be furthered a divisive

[2] "Primary Needs of Young Children": Ner Littner, M.D. Child Welfare League of America, Edith Lauer Award 1959.
[3] Op. cit. Ner Littner, M.D.

or conflicting element for him in how he views his own family. Sometimes it is the religious orientation of the foster family that sharpens this.

Sammy, whose mother is in a mental hospital and who in his first nine years with her suffered seriously from her erratic and bizarre behavior, is now preparing for his bar mitzvah. His father visits him regularly in the foster home and there is seemingly an all-round acceptance of all the individuals involved (Sammy, his own father and older brother, and his foster family, including their son two years older than Sammy). Sammy is struggling to be worthy in his bar mitzvah preparation service of the accolades accorded his foster brother. His father, when the plan for Jewish education was discussed with him soon after Sammy's placement with the foster family three years earlier, accepted the agency's plan with a shrug of indifference. If Sammy wants it, okay. To him it was all nonsense! Now, however, with the actual bar mitzvah imminent—which he and other members of Sammy's family are to attend—he will witness that it is Sammy's foster father who is called up to read from the Torah and it is he who may well be the chief recipient of whatever Kudos are accorded by virtue of Sammy's performance. For Sammy this may sharpen his status as foster child and also the fact that his father can't perform as does his foster father.[4]

Thus the worker, unless aware of the dynamics inherent in this process of religious identification, may overlook working with the parent on this development for his child, which may intensify the implications of separation for father and child, increase the threat to the father's role as parent, and perhaps leave the child with his possible conflict of loyalties and confused identifications.

[4] "Some Traumatic Effects of Separation and Placement": Ner Littner, M.D., Child Welfare League of America Monograph, October 1956, p. 12.

In Avram, almost 20, we see another illustration of the quest
of the disturbed youngster to fill the emotional void; we see,
too, the intensification thereby of separation from his own
family. Avram, third generation American of a completely
assimilated family, Jewish only in designation, spent his first
12 years with a seriously mentally ill mother in and out of
the home of her aging parents from whom she never separated.
In Avram's early years, the father was also only sporadically in
the home, and since the divorce he is completely out. By age
12, Avram and his brother, 14 months younger, had developed
so many problems they could no longer be cared for by the
grandfather and seriously ill grandmother. They were placed
in our treatment residence: Pleasantville. There Avram
became the close friend of a very orthodox youngster who
contributed to Avram's continuing search for God, begun years
earlier when this very bright and imaginative boy had launched
into extensive readings that had already led him to a choice of
orthodoxy. From his Pleasantville friend he learned more about
orthodox ritual and practices, to which he immediately began
to adhere. After three years in Pleasantville, his increasingly
bizarre behavior led to his commitment to a State Mental
Hospital from which two years later he was referred for foster
home placement. At our psychiatric clinic his adherence to
orthodoxy was seen as meeting a deep need and the choice of
a very orthodox home, a Yeshiva and extra tutoring encompassed this component which was so significant for Avram. In
part, because of this religious orientation, it was inadvisable
that Avram return to his own grandfather, already caring for
the younger brother who was in some ways more difficult than
Avram. Having Avram live with them would create far too
many conflicts, although they respect his religious practices and
are grateful that Avram has found a way of living in the world
outside of a hospital, even though on a psychologically mar-

ginal basis. For Avram, as for other youngsters, the development of a firm religious identification is a crucial component in his coping with himself and the world.

There are illustrations involving formalized Hebrew education. However, the ethics of the family, and the ambience of the foster home in daily living are perhaps even more significant considerations: ritualistic practices may highlight these. Differences in the foster family's observances of such holidays as Passover or Chanukah may carry much emotional overtone. The child who prefers to stay with his foster family on Jewish holidays or prefers to go to his own family always requires sensitive handling with the individuals involved.

The basic problem is that our children, so few of whom have had opportunity to develop primary identification, have continuing difficulties in their own identity and in identifications. These difficulties are revealed in unsatisfactory and unsatisfying relationships, often characterized by vacillation and superficiality. Inherent is the lack of development of the underlying substance for continuity and relatedness. Because religion is so emotionally laden, its significance and dynamics must not be overlooked. Yet often it is—because it is seen as a taken-for-granted child rearing responsibility. Among the value differences between the child's own family and foster family which can contribute to conflict and confusion, that of Jewish practice and identity can be significant. This problem is of course seen at its sharpest in those children of mixed marriages who cannot adhere to one or another religion. At one of our girls' residences, Annie alternately wore a Cross or a Mogen David, which she chose to wear was a signal of the quality, at the time, of her relationship with the Agency or with her family. There were times when she wore both together.

There is another observation which should be made :

The status of being a foster child is not one totally accepted in our community. He is often looked upon as the stranger, the inferior, and therefore to a degree suspect. Sometimes this lack of acceptance gets confused in his own mind with his Jewishness, to which may well be added his own feelings of little self-worth. Then the community attitude, intensifying his own feelings about himself, propels him to go wherever he may gain acceptance, which may place him at variance with family, religion, or society.

Addendum : A problem which must be considered — and it is not a complete non-sequitur — is caused by the increasing number of lower middle class Jewish families now moving into Suburbia. An increasing number of our foster families now live there and we are receiving, not enough, but a fair number of applications from suburban residents. Yet we repeatedly face an anomolous situation here. Synagogues, temples readily accept our children for enrollment in religious schools, but frequently we hesitate until we can get acceptance for the foster family's children too. But our foster families, which are eager to enroll their children and join themselves, often find this impossible because of the high fees. Foster families have indicated their hesitancy to plead poverty or request scholarships, have often expressed to us their unwillingness to pay their share in keeping with their income and responsibilities. I bring this here with the question whether just as social agencies have to serve persons of varying incomes — and do so by sliding fee scales — does not the religious institution have a similar responsibility?

A SYMPOSIUM

by
Dr. Hector Ritey

a

The Importance of Religion in the Residential Treatment
of Emotionally Disturbed Children

When we mention "emotionally disturbed children," we
speak of a broad and heterogeneous category. Some children
show from the beginning — and more so from puberty on — a
set of definite emotional disturbances. These range from well-
characterized symptoms to personality problems, and are
expected to be carried on in adulthood. For other children,
the presenting problem is their inability to live at the level of
expectation in their scholastic achievements: their poor performance contradicts their recognizable potential intelligence.
Finally, we have the wide spectrum of behavioral problems,
ranging as far as criminality.

Is there some condition that all these disturbed children
share, so that we can speak with sufficient focalization of one
underlying cause that we find in each of those cases, no matter
how varied the symptomatology may be?

The common denominator exists, and can be summed up
in one brief sentence: there is a gap within that needs to be
filled. To understand how the gap originates, we must go back
to the age level when the child begins acquiring some autonomy
from the mother's over-embracing protection. The chronolog-
ical age, as a rule, can be established between the end of the
second and of the third years. Up to then, the mother's, or
mother substitute's, omnipotence is a reality that spells life
or death to the child. Two years are necessary for the neuro-
muscular unit to be physiologically developed to the extent

of allowing the organism to be a completely functioning physiological unit so that the representation of the "ego," the psychological unit, can follow. In that period of the child's life, the requirement is that the child's exchange with the environment, physical as well as emotional, be geared to an excess of taking, over giving. All the surplus that the child can muster must be diverted to his own problem of physical growth, of acquiring the notions of space and time, and of starting the long and painful process of becoming aware of the limits between himself and the nearest human beings. The problem of human relationships is still many years away.

The child who is in the process of outgrowing this phase of his development is then driven to the ensuing phase. This is the awareness of the existence of other children, and from there he goes on to associate with them. Here, one of the most essential changes takes place. The give-and-take balance, in the relationship with contemporaries, must be a break-even one. The child is exposed to the fact that the choice is between forfeiting the sheltered parent-child tie, where the child is necessarily on the receiving end alone, or of forfeiting the new experience of venturing in the world of contemporaries where the next child has as many rights and demands as he has. This is also the condition that eventually will teach the child the limit of his individuality and hence the bridge to other individuals. The pleasure principle is interfered with in any case; the child is not comfortable while he is giving up the easygoing phase of being overprotected. Nor would he feel comfortable in subjecting his newly acquired powers, which grow daily by sheer physiological action, to limitations that tie him to a past age level.

The possible developments from here on can be numbered by the thousands, and the most improbable of all are total acceptance or total rejection of the new status. Few are even the adults who in some devious or partial or symbolic ways don't have some carry-over or some nostalgic return to that period of practically no responsibility. But the child, much closer to the shock of his reached autonomy, goes through a long series of puzzling experiences. This is the real test of birth — the severage of the nutritional dependency on the mother image — and it does not decay automatically like the umbilical cord.

The first thing that the child realizes is the existence of the unknown. The next child's will and performance is an unpredictable quantity. The autonomy, in the process of being reached, leaves the child to cope with his own devices against hypothetical dangers. It is inherent to that period of life that "unknown" and "dangerous" are by definition equated. This excess of defensiveness is very often carried on in adulthood and manifested as askance of the opposite sex — besides being the deep underlayer of any form of racial or religious intolerance. In the developing child, it creates a vacuum. There is a period in a child's life in which the child feels as though he is hanging in mid-air. He is no longer relying on the all-encompassing protection of the adult; he is not yet attuned to the demands of his growing condition, and he is emotionally divided between his increasing potential capacities and the apprehension of what his steadily increased power means in terms of being exposed to new mysteries and new potential unknown dangers. This conflict, and this feeling of being suspended among mysterious dangers, is in itself not pathological. Pathology begins when it is misplaced over an age level at which it should be progressively outgrown.

In the adult, security is the ability to face the unknown; in the child it is the ability to shun it, or at least to face it with some tangible and well-known defense to fall back upon. The telling line between the two sets of feelings is abstract thought, the device through which one is aware that the unknown can eventually be drawn into the category of the known. Because the development of abstract thought in the child parallels his growing sense of self-reliance, the two attributes can either grow simultaneously, or be stopped or distorted in the same vicious cycle. But at this junction the old sense of belonging (no longer passive as in infancy), is the saving grace. Children and adults alike cannot venture in society, or in their own mental abstraction, unless they feel that their emotions are rooted in something wider than their personalities, which tie them to mankind. A plant, even if perfect in every part, dies if its roots are severed from the ground. A human being, even if potentially untouched, withers away if his emotional life is not rooted in some wider entity wherein he belongs.

The role of the family–religion team is so defined : the roots, the sense of belonging. A vacuum is the alternative. The suicidal drive, which Freud called "the death instinct," looms as a lesser evil when the anxious and obsessive question, "What was I born for?" cannot be answered. The line of defense against the unconscious suicidal drive, which can be safely taken for granted in almost every human being, is to use any conceivable expediency to bridge the vacuum. But expediency is far from being an unavoidable pitfall. Its antagonist is the emotional root of the family–religion team, the rock-bottom of the sense of security.

Religion is really ingrained in a child's mind when it is taught in the family; conversely, family ties without the benefit of religious background are an unstable bulwark, expendable at the earliest request for a compromise. The role of religious symbols and religious practices in the family is paramount and irreplaceable. At an age in which the child is visual, direct, and learns only from tangible experiences, he is exposed to symbols that command the undivided respect of the omnipotent adult. When, in later years, he will be able to absorb abstract concepts, the idea that life has a wider significance that the daily tangible experience will not be alien to his mind, because it will graft itself on an emotional experience that he carries from the years preceding his capacity for abstract thought. To explain with a comparison : the notion of being kind to animals, as a moral precept, is meaningful to those children who learned to love their pet in the age of tangible and concrete experiences.

Religious education, as prophylaxis of childhood emotional upheavals, parallels and complements the religious practices of the family environment. Education is the unfolding of the human potential. Above and beyond its practical value as training for vocation or profession, education is the human link between generations that insures the continuity with the past and heralds the opening toward the future. It climaxes the three attributes of the human condition, inasmuch as it uses two of them — articulate language and abstract thought — to enhance the most essential one : the self-propelling capacity. Education is valuable not so much for what it teaches as for what it stimulates.

Religious education is the mainstay of security. It is the antagonist of the gap of insecurity from which emotional disturbances in childhood emanate, because its scope is boundless. Contrary to the distorted opinion of many self-styled free thinkers, religious education is the most free-minded approach to the need of the youngsters, because it has no value except inasmuch as it is freely understood and accepted. The formal school trains young people for their chosen vocation, but it cannot dwell on teaching its deeper meaning. Work stabilizes in adulthood the rational approach to give in excess of taking. It is in the province of religious education to reveal the teleological meaning of work and of knowledge, its significance in terms of continuity in time, space and depth, and how every human activity branches into a much broader aim than the immediate and practical goal. The youngster who absorbs this concept is beyond the point of no return that would make him regress, in self-defense, to the emotional level of feeling suspended in mid-air between the fear of the unknown and the nostalgic desire for returning to the level of the complete dependency of infancy. When the point of no return is past, the very foundation for emotional deviations of any description and for any kind of objectionable or self-destructive behavior has ceased to exist.

The role of the parents essentially hinges on flexibility. When the child is the pacemaker, and the parent–child relationship is molded to the reality of the child's growth instead of being statistically tied to an immutable pattern of authority, the religious significance of the continuity of mankind is preserved. Dynamics is the key word of any religious manifestation, because man is relentlessly engaged in the conquest of a deeper knowledge of God. The Fifth Commandment is given to the parents as much as to the children : "Thou shalt deserve to be honored by your child." The implementation of the Commandment is the parents' responsibility, since the easiest feeling for every child is to love and honor his parents. If the child's natural feelings were unhampered, the Fifth Commandment would be redundant. Parents approach the child with a true spirit of human mission to the extent that their cooperation is a real partnership. The perfect relation between parents is the climax of whatever has preceded the marriage, so that the religious spirit insures the continuity of the constructive attitude from one generation to the next.

The role of the Jewish religion in this frame can be understood when we consider, first and uppermost, the historical role that Judaism played in the history of mankind. The concept of the One God stands for the end of childhood and the beginning of adolescence of mankind as a whole. Monotheism, and with it the prohibition of images, stands for the reached capacity to conceive the Divinity in terms of abstract thought

—without the crutch of concrete images, of personified gods, and of idols. The One God who freed the Hebrew people from bondage in Egypt drew the line between what was at that time the most progressive people of the pagan world and of the new world, who knew no bondage.

The One God is conceivable only by those human beings who have a unified and harmonic conception of their own selves. This is why, in addition to freedom from the bond of slavery in Egypt, the people of God freed itself of His own inner bondages and crossed the ditch between childhood and adolescence. The human condition began unfolding with more speed and purposefulness when one of the cardinal attributes of the human condition—abstract thought—became the medium of the man–God partnership. Every development from there on, however modified by history and by institutions, even by distortions, is Judaic in essence.

As long as the whole world will not be entirely conquered for monotheism—and in spirit, not only in empty words or in misunderstood formalism—the Jewish people will not disappear, and the pagans, however disguised, will never be stronger than God's will. "And Thy word broke their sword." Within each individual, as in world's history, God's word breaks the sword, in this case the destructive effect of a crystallization to an age level that should have been outgrown, comparable in history to mentality and institutions reminiscent of the pagan era. It behooves the Jewish educator to stress the double meaning that religious education has to every Jewish child. Every Jew is born with an historic mission and a set of duties that he can forfeit only at the cost of some distortion that, sooner or later, in a larger or a lesser amount, will reflect on his emotional stability and on his mental capacity to be at the par with his potential. History, as well as any set of individual problems, is a part of each human being's personality.

In summary, religion plays a preponderant role in the prevention of childhood emotional and mental conditions, and a necessary complementary role in the process of therapy. Because the main goal of psychiatry is prevention rather than cure, so that in the long run cure can be limited to the few unavoidable failures, the teamship between religion and psychiatry is one of the greatest conquests of the decade.

b

The Jewish Component in Residential Treatment

by
Jack Adler,

Chief Psychiatric Social Worker, Hawthorne Cedar Knolls
School of Jewish Board of Guardians of New York

Dr. Ritey sketched out the broad panorama of psycho-social maturation, the role of religion and the particular contribution that Judaism can make to healthy personality development. To this should be added a necessary condition which is essential if the Jewish component is to become a meaningful aspect of the residential treatment center. This involves its acceptance, its practice, and its integration in the total residential treatment program.

Dr. Ritey identified a common element among emotionally disturbed children as "the gap within that must be filled." This "gap" is extensive among the emotionally disturbed children placed in a residential treatment center. This "gap" undoubtedly originates early in a child's life. The first breach occurs within the period when, according to Erik Erikson, the "sense of basic trust" develops. He considers this the cornerstone of a healthy personality and he defines it as "an attitude toward oneself and the world derived from the experiences of the first year of life."[1] It is basic to normal development during the subsequent life stages which characterize the evolvement of the other crucial components of personality—the sense of autonomy of will, of initiative, industry and identity. These are transmitted to the child through the significant inter-personal relationships, first in his family and then through the more extensive relationships outside of it.

Children in residential treatment centers have lacked such wholesome social experiences. "The family–religion team," which according to Dr. Ritey provides the sense of security and of identity for a child, fills the gap of inner emptiness and provides the bridge from narcissism to constructive social involvement, has failed these children, either by its non-existence or by faulty "team work." Such inadequate fusion of family and religion may be exemplified by disturbed children from orthodox Jewish families where the elements of Judaism were ingrained in their homes but its "cultural carriers," the parents, lacked the capacity to represent and to transmit them to their children. The numbers of such children who require residential treatment is relatively small.

I recall one family where observance of orthodox rituals was strictly adhered to and Jewish education insisted upon. All three children, ranging in age from 6 to 12 years, are now in placement; one at Hawthorne, one in Pleasantville and one in a foster home. Among the adolescent boys and girls in residential treatment from such families, most seem in conflict with their family traditions. In their flight from the pathological family relationships they tend to reject their Jewishness. All of them had serious learning and behavior difficulties in the Yeshivas they attended. The girls preferred non-Jewish "boy

[1] Erik H. Erikson, "Growth and Crisis of the Healthy Personality," C. Kluckholm, Henry Murray, D. Schneider, ed. *Personality in Nature, Society and Culture,* N.Y., A. Knopf, 1956, pp. 55–56.

friends." In these families, a mature religious potential was present; a mature parent was lacking.

Most of the Jewish children who inhabit the residential treatment centers have neither experienced the strong religious element nor maturity in their parents. Here, we find great lack or total absence of identity with Judaism, its teachings, and traditions.

To paraphrase Erikson, the important question is — "Do religion and tradition as living psychological forces create the kind of faith and conviction which permeates a parent's personality and thus reinforces the child's basic trust in the world's trustworthiness?" This seems to him to be an essential universal condition for healthy child development. He states that "Whosoever says he has religion must derive a faith from it which is transmitted to infants in the form of basic trust; whoever claims that he does not need religion must derive such faith from elsewhere."[2]

Is this not applicable to the residential treatment center as well? The emotionally disturbed children who reside in it have lacked the life experiences which would have transmitted to them a sense of self-worth, and of confidence in others, a sense of achievement and identity. If their emotional health is to be restored, substitute sources must be available to fill the emptiness and feelings of worthlessness created by their sense of mistrust and diffusion of identity. The residential treatment center which has been entrusted with the task of their rehabilitation must supply this. Its therapeutic function which is the raison d'être of its existence is basically a therapeutic child rearing responsibility with a built-in objective of restoring a healthier child to a healthier home, if he has one, or to the community if he has no family.

The residential treatment center is involved in a continuing struggle with children's pathology, with their symptoms,

[2] Ibid, pp. 64–65.

defensive systems and resistance to change. No adult is spared including the rabbi or religious representative. All become objects of suspicion, and of pathological transference projections. The religious program may have an easier time with the younger child who is more attracted to ritual and holiday celebration and singular adolescent girls may become devotees of the rabbi and his educational endeavors. In general however, the disturbed child has a basic distrust of adults who, for the most part, are viewed as frightening or tyrannical authority whom he must avoid or fight. This is particularly true of adolescents.

All of us who have association with adolescents, professionally and/or as parents, know the personal and interpersonal struggles they experience and the trials they represent for adults. They often appear to be "walking contradictions." There is within them restlessness and confusion, aggressive self assertion and dependent clinging, idealism and rigid conservatism, enthusiasm fluctuating with apathy or what seems to adults, laziness and lack of responsibility. These characteristics represent the so-called "normal" adolescent in his striving to add meaning to his life and to consolidate a sense of identity.

The adolescents in a residential center have seldom reached this stage of constructive instability. They have fought and lost battles in many areas of life including school, home, work, and social relationships. They suffer from insecurities and poor impulse control. They have attempted to overcome their low self-image by either joining with others to fight the adults and their imposed realities, with which they cannot cope, or may have withdrawn into a life of fantasy, characterized by social purposelessness and wasted potential. They distrust, feel unloved as well as unlovable. Even when they seem to be a cohesive gang, they are basically uninvolved and alienated from significant social relationships. Before they are ready to permit themselves to trust, and thus restore the necessary sense of trust in themselves and in others they will test the adults around them to the limit of their capacities. The hazardous road to their recovery must, therefore, be guided by adults with empathy rather than sympathy, strength and firmness rather than hostility or seductiveness, with belief and dedication to developing their potential rather than intellectualization about their pathology.

The residential treatment center, through its "therapeutic milieu" (particularly cottage living) lays the groundwork for change and provides the opportunities for positive activities, relationships, and identifications; individual and group therapy helps the children re-examine and work through previously distorted identifications and their struggles with current ones; the educational and recreation programs add to the sense of mastery and achievement learning, and in play, educational and vocational goals; the religious component can contribute to the acquisition of constructive values and the enrichment of the sense of identity. This tapestry of residential treatment maintains a dynamism and vibrancy in its therapeutic form through adult–child participation. Child involvement through active meaningful participation in all aspects of the residential treatment program is essential if any of its components is to achieve its objectives. They cannot simply be adult-imposed and adult-dominated. They must involve the children in a continuing individual and group process of planning and working together under adult guidance, and they must be differentiated in terms of the children's readiness and capacities. If the religious program, for example, is either rigidly imposed or the children are simply passive recipients of ritual and sermon, it is sterile.

What has been said earlier about the "family–religion team" applies to the personnel of the residential treatment center. Religion, in general, and in our case Judaism in particular, can provide guidelines for the adults in their task of constructively rearing and educating children; it can contribute to children's mature personality integration and achievement of "ego identity," and it has the potential of becoming an important component of the armamentarium of the residential treatment center in its rehabilitative efforts with emotionally disturbed children.

An evaluation of its significance in a residential treatment program should include the following questions :

Does the residential treatment center utilize to full advantage the cultural and esthetic elements, opportunities and ethical teachings of Judaism?

Does its leadership believe and participate in conveying it to the staff and to the children?

Are its personnel invested in it and do they apply it not only superficially on holidays but in every day living?

Is it applied with sensitivity to the children's capacities and understanding?

Above all, are its ethics integrated within the present life-pattern of the institution? The children are quick to grasp whether the adults practice or only profess a value system. They will learn effectively from both, but only constructively from those adults who, in their own lives and daily comportment, represent the positive values they teach.

There are numerous difficulties that may handicap a Jewish residential treatment center from achieving the full use of the religious component in its treatment program. Among these are difficulties in finding Jewish personnel, especially in the child-care area. A Jewish staff is not always fully identified with Judaism and not always capable of transmitting its values to the children; some centers also accept non-Jewish children for treatment and are staffed by large numbers of non-Jewish personnel. In addition, the difficulties the institution faces are not only internal but external as well. It is not an "island unto itself" but part of the greater community, which directs and affects it. It cannot exist outside the vortex of the dynamic instability of our culture. The disturbed child is a product of the alienation of the adult in a society which is materialistically rather than spiritually oriented, which no longer provides the closely knit kinship groups, nor the life tempo in which religion was an organic element of daily living.

These are realistic difficulties but they need not be overwhelming or paralyzing. They can be overcome and adaptations achieved to realize the constructive contribution Judaism has to offer to the rehabilitation of emotionally disturbed Jewish children. The Jewish component is only one aspect, one element of the overall human and cultural gestalt that we adults in residential treatment represent to the children whose rehabilitation and rearing have been entrusted to us. Each component of the residential treatment program is important. A weakness in one reflects upon and weakens the whole edifice of residential treatment. Support and dedication must encompass all of them.

The Jewish component can become a meaningful contributor to the residential treatment center if it is an accepted element in its treatment philosophy, if it is practiced and not just professed by its personnel, and if it is provided with the psychological and physical conditions that will attract children to its esthetically beautiful rituals, historical traditions, and its intellectually challenging, and ethically ennobling offerings.

c

Comments on Dr. Ritey's Paper on the Theme — The Jewish Component in Residential Treatment

by
Rabbi Jack Bemporad

The child who comes to Hawthorne Cedar Knolls School for residential treatment has, in most cases, already been involved, either institutionally or privately, with some psychiatric or other type of care. This other care has ended in failure. Apart from having a major problem the child has experienced continuous failure in his coping with this problem, and his style of life has adjusted itself to failure and all that is associated with failure. The child's home, in most cases, is also one where the parents have been unable to cope with their problems. Many of our children come from broken homes, many are the children of former inmates of concentration camps, and a large percentage are adopted. Where the child comes from an intact family — which apparently functions normally, in many of these cases — the normality of the family is at the expense of the child. The child here functions as a scapegoat.

The religious background of our children is also one that may be characterized as a failure. In most cases the child's religious identification is extremely confused and warped. Where the child is the product of a mixed marriage or an inter-racial marriage, religious identification is very often connected with parental acceptance and rejection. In many of these cases the children seek conversion as a means of identification with the parent or for acceptance on the part of the parent. Usually, where the child comes from an inter-married couple, there is great confusion and indefiniteness as to his religious status. Among the boys we have close to 20 per cent who come from families who are inter-married. Among the girls it is close to 50 per cent.

The vast majority of our children, 80 per cent among the girls and 70 per cent of the boys at Hawthorne Cedar Knolls School, come from families where religion is, at most, a form. They are not members of a congregation; generally they do not observe any religious practices whatsoever. Where there has been some observance, the symbols associated with these observances have become repugnant to these children. Religion has been used in a self-defeating and destructive manner by the family. It would seem that the Jewish symbols should be directed towards Jewish values, but for many of our children these symbols are associated with the hypercritical attitude of the parents.

What role can religion play in a residential treatment center, where at best the children are totally ignorant and confused as to their Jewishness, and at worst openly hostile and rebellious? This is the question as it faces us practically. So far we have only discussed the problem in respect to the children and their families. There is, perhaps, an even greater problem in respect to the staff at these institutions. I think the day is over when the social worker is openly hostile to religion, yet in most agencies an overwhelming necessity to survive in a pathological milieu is so pressing that religion, if not idealogically rejected, is practically swept aside. It can, then, only function on the periphery. An overburdened staff with continuous "emergency situations" finds itself functioning always in "crisis" and thus makes it difficult for a religious program. The Midrash has God telling Moses, "The Egyptians are coming and you are prolonging the prayers, make your prayers short." When there is little money and an inadequate staff, where stability is a goal and not a fact, the underlying support that is needed for a religious program is non-existent and the

program suffers. The Director of Religious Education finds
himself isolated with people willing to cooperate but finding it
difficult because of other pressures and needs.

It was clear from my very first year at Hawthorne Cedar
Knolls School that the boys and girls responded differently to
the religious program. After considerable study we discovered
that the boys viewed religion in social terms, hence it was
important for the boys to have the proper identification, to be
proud of their Judaism. For instance, the bar mitzvah ceremony more and more took on the form of the individual
achievement in terms of his social relationship. In some cases
the bar mitzvah was symbolic of the child's public mastery of
religious materials, and it signified an achievement as a Jew
among Jews. We thus emphasized the aspect of belonging
to an age-old religious community; we stressed his sense
of belonging to the Jewish people and his identification
with the values of that people. With the girls this approach
failed completely. The girls see their religion in mainly personal terms. They viewed it from the standpoint of belief and
self-transformation. The Confirmation class for girls more and
more concerned itself with clarifying religious belief. It investigated the meaning of faith; how one can believe in God. I
found more and more that one reached the girls if one under-
played the social and historic elements of Judaism and emphasized the personal and theological elements. The girls were
searching for a religious identity, the boys for a religious
justification.

The religious program has to develop a style of life on the
part of the children, one that has continuity and is constantly
reinforced by the environment. What is needed is a continuing
religious program embodying weekly religious services and
classes; weekly youth programs such as B'nai Brith Girls and
A.Z.A., which will eventually make a religious change. Most
of all the Jewish component in residential treatment can be

transmitted only if the children are exposed to significant adults on the staff who are positively identified with Judaism. We must transmit to the child not only our faith in him and in his future, but our belief in the teachings of Judaism and our faith in God. The rabbi cannot do it alone.

d

The Jewish Component in Residential Treatment

by
Paul Steinfeld

Resident Director Pleasantville Cottage School,
Jewish Child Care Association of N.Y.

Dr. Ritey makes two points which I can illustrate from my own experience with emotionally disturbed children at Pleasantville Cottage School.

First, concerning the psychological "gap" in their emotional development, many children reveal conflicts arising from an unsatisfied need to rely on the "all encompassing protection of the adult." In simple ways, such as neglecting to wear rubber boots in snowy weather, our children illustrate their failure to take over for themselves the parental responsibility of protection from the weather. Not only will they fail to protect themselves, but when the adults charged with their care, the cottage staff, attempt to remind or persuade or demand that they submit to this form of care or protection, the children resist and evade. The unconscious and repressed hunger for parental protection is denied and indeed the child vigorously defends himself against the parent substitute's attempts to give care. It is much easier for the staff and children when I, as resident director, issue a "rule" that only children with boots may be permitted outdoors on a particular snowy day. In this way the staff member can, in effect, appeal to the child: "Look, I am not trying to care for you (God forbid), I am only trying to follow orders." Even then many children's defenses against their unresolved dependency needs are not conquered, for some will run to me on the campus and try to get me to withdraw the rule, or at least modify it for them. Even in medical emergencies some children fight bedcare which is so symbolic of the absent mother's responsibility. Other children with opposite defenses are continually seeking the nurse's attention for imagined illnesses. I could go on with many other illustrations.

The second point I wish to illustrate is how religious education outside the family helps nurture the individual and enables him to bridge this gap in his emotional development and to conceive of a past and a future. How in the residential treatment center do we use religious education to further the emotional development of a child who has alienated himself from his group and from his society? This is done by making religious values a part of the value system of the institution. That is, the staff in their relationships with children and one another must convey qualities of understanding, patience, forgiveness, justice, and other standards of decent human behavior and orderly existence. In addition, these religious values are related to the historic identity of the child through symbols and ceremonies which the child can see, hear, feel, and taste.

The child comes to us with his own notions of what is supremely important. Usually these are the material things necessary for his existence. Usually the child lacks the stock onto which we might graft the idea that life has other values than its daily tangible aspects and immediate gratifications. Only when the child experiences with some adult first a freedom from old conflict, and then a kind of relationship which challenges his old values, can he begin to conceive of a God whose attributes are justice, mercy and compassion, creativity, and all those qualities which make us distinctively human. But there is still a gulf between the abstract concept of religion and a religious identity. Many disturbed children are expert in using abstract reasoning power to strengthen their defenses against personal involvement in one or another aspect of the institution's program. We are familiar with the ingenious "lawyers" who lose no opportunity to evade various forms of responsibility in the institution. In order to achieve a personal identity, the individual must have a "local habitation and a name." It is this which we attempt to supply at Pleasantville through the Jewish character of the institution.

Before the child enters he is aware that he is coming to the Jewish Child Care Association. Occasionally the child demonstrates his resistance to placement right there — objecting that he is not really Jewish and therefore should not live in a Jewish institution even though he has two Jewish parents. Many routines identify the institution as Jewish. On the Sabbath and holidays, aside from synagogue attendance, the food, clothing, and schedule of activities are different. Bar mitzvah and bat mitzvah celebrations are an important part of cottage life. Various symbols of Jewish tradition and Jewish educational materials are prominently displayed in cottages and other buildings. Different art forms are used to enhance the child's awareness of Jewish festivals. We are known in the community as a Jewish institution and a local synagogue uses our classrooms on Sundays for their religious school. The child cannot fail to perceive that he is living in a Jewish environment and therefore the religious values of the institution are specifically related to him as a member of this group.

To what extent does this Jewish character of the treatment center help with the child's problem of alienation, which is a symptom of his developmental gap? I cannot give a statistical report of this, but I have an impression based on contact with many children during their residence and sometimes after their departure. One boy writing from a naval vessel forcefully and touchingly describes the importance for him in being able to participate with other Jewish sailors in religious services. He considered this a critically important experience and he paid tribute to his training at Pleasantville, which alone had enabled him to participate in these services. We know that many children and their parents find bar mitzvah or bat mitzvah very meaningful and are willing to invest much effort in preparing for this ceremony. Most of the children display great curiosity about their Jewish heritage and a general interest in religion, even when they are unable to invest much in formal study of this or other subjects. Rather frequently we find that the child who most loudly voices his protest against any religious identity actually hides a deep hunger for it. The same boy who did not want to come to a Jewish institution expressed an urgent need to talk with our director of Jewish Education soon after his arrival. He had many questions about Judaism. A girl who belligerently announced that she was not Jewish or religious later decided that she wished to prepare for bat mitzvah. Now her affirmation of Jewishness has become as vigorous as her previous denial.

My experience with the children therefore convinces me that while many reveal difficulty in achieving a comfortable religious identity, they also have a great need for it. In a milieu that contains different religious values from those the child knew previously, he begins to question his old values but may be unable to choose new ones. The particular symbols, ceremonies, and practices of a religious group help establish his unique identity and his legitimate inheritance of new religious values.

RELATIONSHIP OF THE ADULT CHILD TO THE AGED PARENT

by
Gerald Beallor
Supervisor, Jewish Family Service

Our interest in, and concern for, the aging has increased in recent years, as we have become aware of the ever-increasing numbers of men and women past 60 in our community and throughout the nation. At Jewish Family Service, where we have developed a special service to help the aged, we serve an ever-increasing number of aged persons and their families — currently at the rate of 5,000 applications a year. What do we see from our vantage point? What conclusions can be drawn from our experiences with this large number of families?

Perhaps the most significant aspect of our work with the aged stems from the fact that aged people wish to continue to live in the community wherever possible. However, to do so many of them need various kinds of support. The need for help in part comes from the fact that aging is often accompanied by factors related to the health of the individual or his place in society that are unique to the aged person. Illness, or the fear of illness and incapacitation, senility, inadequate housing, lack of sufficient financial resources, and a feeling of uselessness burden many aged persons. Furthermore, their change of status in the family, as adult children move away, coupled with changes in the neighborhoods in which they live, frequently result in loneliness and isolation. Friends die off, sometimes a spouse also; children move to distant parts of the nation. The result is to stretch the less resilient capacity of the older person to adjust in his home. A most important aspect of this is the fact that these difficulties result in aggravating conflicts which previously existed or were foreshadowed in the earlier relationships of the aged to their family and community.

Generational conflicts are increased and marital conflict is more to the forefront. With these problems weighing heavily, children or aging parents come to Jewish Family Service for help.

While the plight of those aged who are most alone and isolated, and frequently ill and unattended provides dramatic evidence of the special problems of the aged; nevertheless, in this presentation I would like to address myself primarily to those aged persons and couples who have raised families of their own and now are the parents of adult children. Here we are faced with not only a complex social situation but unresolved moral and ethical problems related to our concepts of the duties of children to their parents as well as vice versa. Not only are our own traditions somewhat contradictory in this area but in addition, the way in which we live as a people tends to exaggerate and worsen conflict between the generations. Our ancient Biblical heritage carries a clear enunciation of the responsibility of the child for his aged parent. The provision of honor and respect, as well as support, is frequently reiterated. Yet, on the other hand, there is the famous story of the Jewish wise woman, who describes the flight of the eagle over the stormy sea with its eaglet at its side. The eaglet begins to founder and the father carries the baby in its claws. They fly low, over the raging sea, with the wind and the water tearing at them. The eagle is near exhaustion, turns to the eaglet and states that he hopes that when its eaglet becomes an adult, it will remember its father's sacrifice for him and care for him, etc. The eaglet's response to the father is to say he cannot promise this, that the most he can promise is that when he is an adult he will care for his children as well as his father has cared for him. Just as this problem is posed in our tradition, so is it also posed in the changing way of life as it is lived today.

Seldom does it occur that three generations do live under the same roof. Even more important is the fact that today the mobility of families results in early separation of adult children from their parents by the span of states and continents, so that many parents live hundreds and thousands of miles from their adult children and their grandchildren. In such situations difficulties, as they arise, are frequently worsened by the lack of support and communication between generations.

This can best be illustrated through an exposition of some typical situations which come to the attention of Services to the Aged. These are neither the most ill people nor those in greatest need of emergency help, but rather the aged that live in the community and might be members of any of our families.

Recently, a teacher, a mother of two children, visiting from California, requested an interview for herself and her 72-year-old parents, who live in Manhattan. The daughter was very concerned about her father, who no longer leaves his house although he is physically strong and healthy. He had withdrawn from his many club activities and remains at home. He believes he has cancer and other illnesses, although physical examinations have ruled out any serious physical illness. Her father had led an active life until a few years ago. His relationship with his wife was good and he took pride in the success of his daughters and his grandchildren. However, as frequently occurs with the aged, her father underwent surgery for a prostate condition and simultaneously was forced to retire. He has not been the same since, everyone says.

This man's withdrawal into his home caused his wife great anguish. She, herself, was losing her hearing and was in dread of the possibility of becoming deaf. In her fright she lashed out at her husband, who was a ready target, sitting in his armchair at home. The daughter, on her visit from California, found the situation so bad that she sought counsel from a friend of hers who is a psychiatrist. The friend suggested that they come here. where they have since been seen and placed in therapy. This man's loss of his job, along with an operation which challenged his basic feelings about himself as a man, resulted in the symptoms shown and led to breakdown in the basic, marital relationship.

Another family came to us at the point where a son, married and with children, was accepting an excellent employment opportunity in a Southern state. He brought his 63-year-old widowed mother to us for counseling. She was immersed in self-pity and feeling that she was being abandoned. Her own husband passed away about six years ago, and since then she has felt displaced and dislocated. What little funds she was left with were nearly gone because she had made no attempt to become self-supporting. It is evident to everyone that her failure to do anything with herself has been her way of showing her helplessness to her son, in the expectation that he would take her into his own home. When we saw the mother, more of her disappointment was seen in her belief that children owe a great deal to their parents. She still recalls the pain of the children's birth and her anger is turned toward her daughter-in-law, who is blamed for her son's turning away from Judaism. They have become affiliated with a Protestant religion. Further anger and resentment in the family has been caused by the fact that she feels that she has rights as a grand-mother, one of which is to have her grandchildren given a Jew-ish education regardless of their parents' choice. This woman, unless helped in counseling, will live in increasing pain and misery as her dreams of being taken care of become further and further removed from reality. She must be helped to see how she contributes to the tension between herself and her child. She has an insatiable hunger for love and care. Even at this age, she may be able to face this and move out into a life of her own.

The next illustration gives poignant evidence of the deterioration of a good marriage under stress. The loss of skill due to a combination of age and illness and subsequent forced retirement made for a most unbearable situation for a man, whose life had been devoted to his skilled trade in the garment industry. After years of struggling and working at his skill he put together enough to have a small business of his own. Now, following a stroke from which he has pretty well recovered, he no longer has the business and employers will not hire him, even on a part time basis. They and he know that he no longer has his former skill and even when one of them, out of kindness and pity, hires him for a day, he knows that later they have to re-do all the work he has spoiled. This man came with his wife, who sought help because of a terrible conflict between the two during the past year or two. Their children are grown, they have grandchildren, and they enjoy their relationships with them. However, with this man home all the time and his clumsy attempts to be helpful in the house, his wife finds his being around extremely difficult to take. She has never uttered a word in anger to him, fearing that to do so might cause him to have another stroke. Her anger is held within her. The result is that she weeps constantly as she finds him falling short of her ideal when they visit with their friends or have social activities in their home. These disappointments are rightly felt by her husband as criticisms, to which his reaction is to fly into a temper tantrum and throw objects and scream and yell at her. With his confidence undermined and her anger held within her, their long-standing marriage, which had previously seemed adequate, now became almost unbearable. They are now being seen together, as a couple, receiving marital counseling, which can assist them in re-establishing a relationship more comfortable to both of them. Following a brief period of treatment they both became aware of many of their unacceptable feelings and were able to express their anger and anxiety directly to one another. The result was a lessening of the friction and tension between them.

Recently a young woman approached Services to the Aged, asking if we could help with her 67-year-old mother. Her mother came with her for a first visit and it was evident that she was extremely depressed and filled with inner rage. She is above average in intelligence and has demonstrated a good capacity for managing a home and operating in business. This was done when her husband left her and she had to bring up her two daughters. Her whole life became absorbed in raising these girls. She arranged her working hours so that they were never left really alone. She attempted to dominate and control their lives and felt, as they grew older, that few men would be good enough for her daughters. She developed, in particular, an extremely close relationship with one of the girls. When this daughter married she lived near her and helped her in every area of her life. The other daughter remained somewhat more distant. Two and a half years ago, the adored daughter suddenly died. The mother went into mourning, from which she has not yet emerged. However, what is most important is the fact that she now is trying to have the second daughter become to her what the other one was, an expectation which is impossible and has led to such severe arguments and friction between them that they are seldom able to see one another. To this second daughter, the mother seems critical and interfering. In addition, the mother feels that this daughter's husband does not take adequate care of this daughter and this has furthered the strife. The only time this woman seems to be happy is when she is at work. She will need a considerable period of help from one of the caseworkers in Services to the Aged, to assist her in working through the loss she feels, of the adored daughter in whom she invested so much, and to help her establish a more realistic and sound relationship with the remaining daughter and her grandchildren.

A retired couple in their 60's came at the advice of the family physician. Both are successful adults and parents, each having done well in their chosen professions and with their families. They are now at a point in their lives where both have retired but continue in professional activities on a basis which is pleasing to both of them, since it is no longer required that they go to work. What should then be the happiest period of their life has been saddened by the unexpected death of one of their sons. The daughter-in-law and the grandchildren are doing quite well. However, the parents have tried to be "too helpful" and have sought to assist beyond anything requested of them, and it was their daughter-in-law who consulted the family physician about the parents' interference. When he referred them to us, he told us he felt that they were obsessed with guilt and therefore needed constantly to get involved in daughter-in-law's life. The effect on the older couple has been for each to resent the other's lack of attentiveness and consideration. Their activities outside the home have diminished and their sense of satisfaction about their lives is gone. They are being helped, in group therapy, to reconstitute their own marriage and relationship with one another.

What is significant in these illustrations of aged parents in conflict with themselves and their adult children is that the concerns they have for one another can so evidently turn to hurt and anger when there is a lack of understanding arising from changes in the basic situations in which these people live. Death, illness, loss of livelihood, retirement, movement to another state; all of these upset the balance in the family's equilibrium. Most of these families faced other crises in the past, which temporarily changed the balance, but they were younger and more resilient and could meet them as they arose. Very often, meeting them left them stronger and better able to cope with life as it was presented later. However, as these people have passed 60 or 70, their resiliency has decreased. They can no longer muster the resources to carry through the crisis without outside help, such as Jewish Family Service offers. The support may be temporary or over a long period of time, but is necessary, if they are to maintain sufficient health to remain in the community. Frequently, much can be done for these families that will not only restore them to better functioning, but may even help to alleviate problems which have plagued them throughout their lives but with which they have never dealt until this time.

As was indicated in the earlier illustrations, the support and help the aged person needs when in difficulty is offered through the Services to the Aged Division of Jewish Family Service. This service is staffed with skilled family caseworkers, who have had experience and training in various phases of family counseling. In addition, they are specially trained for work with the aged. As with younger members of families, the aged face insuperable difficulties in working out the problems of their lives when they are deeply disturbed and are psychologically unable to adapt to the changes that have come into their lives. We now know that the range of possible new adaptations for aged persons is quite broad, and like all other people, with help, the aged can change considerably so as to cope better with many of the vicissitudes of life. Our therapeutic techniques and methods of treatment are quite similar to those used in family treatment with children and their parents. Counseling the aged calls for fully trained professional caseworkers, with an additional body of knowledge in relation to the aged and an interest and willingness to work with this age group. The caseworker in Services to the Aged is equipped to work with the broadest range of problems presented.

From a preventive point of view, these situations suggest that earlier attention to some of the potential difficulties might have avoided the current difficult situations. Had the woman who wishes to live with her son now been able, or been helped to be able, to be more active in her own life, throughout her marriage, she would not now find it so necessary to be taken care of by her son. The man whose lack of skill is crushing following his stroke would be able to make a far different adjustment if his life had included other satisfying activities in addition to his work.

In general, we can say that any activity of people's lives which contributes to their well-being, satisfaction, and capacity as human beings, will help them as they become older. Furthermore, we can state that our society must begin to make better provision for its aging citizens who require special and better housing and medical resources if they are to remain in the community. The aged want help and can use it. It has been known for a long time that the seriously ill and dependent aged require institutional care. It is only recently that we have come to recognize that the "well" aged, like the rest of us, wish to live in the community and to participate in it. It is up to us to make that possible.

JEWISH CONTENT IN CASEWORK

by
William Posner,
formerly Executive Director of the Jewish Community
Services of Long Island

I wish we could find a substitute for the term "Jewish Content" or for the term "Jewish Component," which is used frequently to define or to describe the peculiarly Jewish elements that enter into our casework process with Jewish clients.

I say this because I feel there is something "outside" about these terms. They seem too much like ingredients sprinkled into a mixture called casework. They are a separate part of the whole, rather than of the whole itself. They are of the outer rather than of the inner.

Dr. Herbert H. Aptekar has recently come out quite strongly for the term "Jewish Casework" to describe the implications of Jewishness for casework process. Dr. Aptekar states:

Let us not bury our heads in the sand and say there is no such thing as Jewish casework, by which we mean, of course, that there is no Jewish *method*. There does not need to be a Jewish method. It is sufficient that there are Jewish people and that these people need to be understood, not just as individuals, not just as Americans, but as Americans with a particular turn of mind, a particular cultural heritage (not the same for all), a particular constellation of common feelings, and a particular quality of experience. This is enough, as I see it, to make for Jewish casework, Jewish center work, and Jewish community organization.

Perhaps the term we use does not matter. What is important is its meaning to us, conceptually and in practice.

For me, Jewish content in casework is a totality. It is part of the Gestalt of casework itself — the methodological structure of helping — as well as inherent in the philosophy of the agency, the practice of the social worker, and the problems brought by the client.

If we had the time, there would be value at this point in relating our concern for Jewish content in casework to the broader implications of religio-socio-cultural factors for casework practice generally, not just in a Jewish agency or with Jewish clients. Suffice it to say that social work as a whole is today giving considerable thought to these questions.

How then do we understand Jewish content in structure and in practice?

The agency, of course, is primary to our consideration. The Jewish social agency is an instrument of the Jewish community. No matter what its function may be the agency represents the Jewish community to the client. Although many clients may come to the Jewish agency for lack of similar non-sectarian services, many clients do choose the agency precisely because it is Jewish. For all clients, in whatever group they fall, the agency's Jewishness has some special meaning. There is the client who expects that because he comes to a Jewish agency his every need or desire will be met regardless of whether the agency is set up for the purpose or not, or whether it feels the client can really be helped with the service. In such cases, the Jewishness of the agency may constitute a problem in helping the client face realistically the limited conditions under which the agency can provide help. There may be other clients who, though not giving expression to it, may be fearful of the particular Jewish ideology the agency may represent, or the demands or expectations the agency may make upon them. The agency's Jewishness may thus intensify that fear.

For another group of clients, the Jewish agency may represent the "conscience" of the Jewish community. For these clients, bringing a problem to the Jewish agency implies that they are disclosing it to the Jewish community which it represents. Such an action might arouse a fear of leaving themselves open to condemnation by the Jewish community. There is shame and guilt; a feeling of running counter to the Jewish tradition.

Philosophically, the agency must be ready to accept all types of clients no matter of what cultural background or religious view.

The worker is the pivotal point, as well as the connecting

link, between the client on the one hand and the agency on the other. If, as we said earlier, the Jewish social agency must be accepting of every segment of Jewish life, it naturally puts the responsibility upon the worker to have some knowledge of, or at least an inquiring mind about religious practices, customs, changing patterns of Jewish family and community living. Perhaps of equal importance is the worker's knowledge and understanding of his own psychological and socio-cultural orientation as it impinges upon the casework relationship.

Although social workers may find it easy to talk about and to accept cultural relativity; that is, the difference that exists among groups or individuals, it is another matter when a person of a different culture comes for help and when we have to develop a close relationship with him. The attitude then is to consider him to be somewhat deviant and the temptation exists to reorient that person in line with our own cultural attitudes. It is difficult for us to accept emotionally that which may run counter to those attitudes that have become part of our own ego and superego structure, for this would represent a denial of ourselves. The culture conflict which results can often create innumerable difficulties in our work with clients. It may lead us at times to consider a cultural difference as an aberration of some sort or it may lead us to a treatment plan which runs counter to the client's own cultural orientation.

I will grant all of this, grant the agency philosophy, the client's desire for religio-cultural understanding, the worker's own understanding of religious practices and customs, and an understanding of his own religio-cultural background. In fact I believe that few social workers would quarrel with this. I think there will be general agreement too that a client who comes to the agency with a problem rooted specifically in Jewishness — such as intermarriage or religious school attendance — requires not only basic understanding by the worker but that the problem itself requires specific understanding in terms of the client's religio-cultural background as well as its psychological implications.

But what about the problem that is not—on the face of it at least—rooted in Jewishness? What about the average marital problem, where the presenting problem is one of incompatability, financial management, divergent interests, job problems? Or the child guidance situation where the problem is lack of school adjustment, inability to make friends, lack of parent–child relationship?

What is Jewish about these problems? What is different about the Jewish agency's approach to these problems than the approach of the non-sectarian agency or child guidance clinic?

My view is that it is different and that even in this type of situation the Jewishness of the agency and Jewish content play a role in the help we give.

I firmly believe that most clients who come to a Jewish agency choose it because it *is* Jewish or if they do not choose it for its Jewishness are psychologically aware of it. I believe that because of this choice or awareness it has a bearing on the client's attitudes and feelings, and that unless the worker injects this element and its meaning to the client, we miss an essential clarifying element in the casework process. I believe firmly that most Jews today—certainly our client group—have a great desire and a great need for group identification as Jews. Whether it is the growth of suburban living, or the lessened need for assimilation, there seems to be a return to, or a clinging to, the Jewish heritage on the part of the young American Jew who represents the greatest number of our clients. He may practice his Jewishness differently than did his parents, but the roots and feelings are there. The psychological implications of the client's Jewishness to the problems he brings are therefore just as basic to our concern as is the psychological meaning of asking for help generally or the meaning of fee to a client.

For casework process this means that I as a worker, having some understanding of the meaning of separation or divorce or family breakup, or the meaning of poor parent–child relationships, or delinquency, or sexual acting out among Jews, or the meaning of negative attitudes of adult children toward aged parents in Jewish tradition — will initiate a discussion of the relationship of the person's Jewishness to the problem. Frequently, one discussion alone, at intake, may be sufficient to bring this to the fore. And even though the client may feel that Jewishness has no bearing on his problem, it will at least give him, as well as the worker, the freedom to get into this area at a later point.

Failure to use the agency's and client's Jewishness deprives us, I believe, of appropriate helping methods. This comes into sharper focus today, particularly, when there is growing emphasis on family diagnosis; on the need to know how people live and act together. Religion, culture, background, heritage are important elements in this framework, for people tend to find expression for their personality and internal needs in the culture of which they are a part, and to project upon specific aspects of their environment and culture their internal conflicts.

I would propose that in addition to the various methods and tools we use to achieve a psycho-social diagnosis in the case-work process, we develop tools and methods to arrive at a religio-cultural diagnosis as well, for to me the latter is as basic as the former.

In this whole area there are at least several complex problems that require basic examination. One is the question of how the Jewish social worker can be all things to all people, to clients of all segments of Jewish philosophy and practice. In effect we are asking the Jewish caseworker to acknowledge as given the philosophy and practice of the Chassid of the Satmar Rebbe on the one hand, and on the other extreme the completely assimilated Jew. We are saying to him : "these are the religious and cultured ways in which Jews live. You must take all of these ways for granted and help only with the client's problem." How can the problem not affect the religious and cultural ways of the clients? Must we stay out of these areas, and how can we really? If in truth a child should not continue in the Yeshiva, or if in our judgment an unaffiliated client might find real companionship in a synagogue — must we stay out of it? If we as social workers have the responsibility of concern for Jewishness do we then not also have the responsibility of making judgments about it — positive or negative? At what point must this be a shared responsibility with the rabbi?

A second question related to the first is the one of conflicting values, or at least what may seem as conflicting between those Jewish values devolving upon the individual Jew to fulfill his responsibility as a member of the group for group survival and social work values — those relating to individual responsibility, self-determination, and self-fulfillment as an individual.

Is flexibility the answer? Does it depend on our interpretation of Jewish values and social work values? Does it depend upon the worker who may or may not be able to go beyond *his* own values? Does it depend on the degree to which a worker can have a objective view of the values of others while yet remaining firm in his own conviction?

Only the Jewish worker in the Jewish agency who is knowledgeable can give the proper answers.

3

Intermarriage

The increasing rate of interfaith marital unions is obviously of acute concern to the Jewish community. The Commission on Synagogue Relations itself conducted a seminal conference devoted to the problem of "Intermarriage and the Future of the American Jew." Intermarriage is a penalty of life in the free and open society of the United States and the change in attitudes of the present Jewish co-educational generation from those of their parents and grandparents.

The entire climate of opinion of young American Jews toward exogamy has changed. Fewer Jewish men and women oppose it, and the increase in the rate of interfaith marriage is a reflection of this fact.

Certainly, as Dr. Eisenstein points out, children whose parents and community agencies have succeeded in imparting to them their Jewish values are more likely to identify themselves with the Jewish people and to marry a member of their own group than those whose parents are marginal or peripheral Jews. Furthermore, the challenge to the Jewish group and the character of its communal life is implicit in intermarriage. Dr. Eisenstein offers a perceptive, insightful guide for Jewish parents in this area of concern to them.

Intermarriage reflects the fact that the Jewish community is not so integrated and cohesive as in the past. It is also more open, permissive, and tolerant than it was in the *shtetl* or European *Kehillah* of years past. The percentage of marginal or peripheral Jews has increased, and the concerns of contemporary Jewish youth are more secular, more materialistic, and more ego-centered than were those of their forbears.

The observations of Solomon Weiss are significant. They are based on a good sampling (140 intermarriages out of 1,067 cases), of the characteristics of Jewish individuals who intermarry and eventually desert. Their first desertion apparently was from Judaism. Since this is the nub of the intermarriage problem, Mr. Weiss' essay offers helpful insights for the community and the synagogue.

Professor Cahnman presents a fascinating, insightful pioneer report of an increasing community problem — interracial marriage and the Negro-Jewish child. The comments by Mrs. Florence Brown add meaningful information on this little known situation.

INTERMARRIAGE : FOR JEWISH PARENTS
by
Ira Eisenstein

A Growing Concern

If you are at all typical of American Jewish parents, you are worried lest your son or daughter marry outside the faith. Whether you are deeply committed to Jewish survival, or

merely concerned with the happiness of your children, you are
aware of the fact that the statistics indicate a growing percentage of intermarriages between Jews and non-Jews; and
since the chances of a Jewish person marrying a non-Jew are
clearly greater than ever before, you undoubtedly give a good
deal of thought to the question. This must be especially true
of you if your child has gone off to college out of town (or
even in town), for you know that their social contacts with
non-Jews are frequent, and they occur in an atmosphere of
intellectual and cultural exploration. College age is the time
when young people are frequently in a state of rebellion against
their parents and home influence; and this encourages them
to seek out companionship among those who represent new
and unfamiliar backgrounds.

Young people are equally aware of the new trends;
yet they seem to be less concerned about intermarriage.
They frequently point to individual instances in which intermarriages have led to happy lives. And if one calls attention
to the fact that such marriages most often (the estimate is 70
per cent) lead to assimilation and estrangement from the
Jewish tradition, the answer is usually a cause of dismay to
those who care about whether Judaism survives or not.
Apparently, most young people today do not seem to be distressed by the thought that a 4,000-year-old tradition is in
danger of disintegration.

They seem to be more interested in their personal happiness
than they are in the future of the Jewish people. And if one
quotes to them the high percentage of cases in which intermarriages have been unsuccessful, they frequently argue that
statistics do not apply to individual situations; it won't
"happen" to them. Besides, they would declare, the reason
intermarriages are fraught with difficulties is that the older
people (yourselves, for example) are still prejudiced against
persons of differing nationality, race, or religion. If it were not

for the social pressures which intermarriages have to contend with, many more of them would succeed. For them, therefore, intermarrying becomes an opportunity to strike a blow for human brotherhood, equality, and freedom. How else, they contend, will humanity attain to unity if people of differing faiths and backgrounds refuse to marry one another?

Why This is Addressed to Parents

That is why this essay is addressed to Jewish parents. You must be prepared to understand your own reluctance to condone (certainly to encourage) mixed marriages. You must be made to realize that intermarriage is not the only way to achieve brotherhood among men. As one distinguished Negro is said to have remarked to a white man: "I don't want to be your brother-in-law. I want to be your brother." Brotherhood is the spirit in which people treat one another, the ethical level of their relationship. It is an ideal of equality and also mutual recognition of dignity. It is not dependent upon establishing *family* relationship. Indeed, all groups have a tendency to marry within their respective groups; they find themselves more at ease with members of their own race or religion or nationality. Even if all barriers were removed, the vast majority of people would freely choose as their mates members of their own social groups.

You should therefore not feel guilty — or allow your children to make you feel guilty — for advocating intermarriage for your children. You will in no way be impeding the progress of mankind. But, on the other hand, you must recognize the fact that rational argument with young adults on matters of this sort is not likely to be of any avail if these young people have not been brought up by you to *feel* the tug of attraction to their own people, and to the Jewish way of life. For this reason, it is important to divide the remainder of this essay into separate sections, each one devoted to a discussion of what needs to be done, and what attitudes need to be adopted, as they are growing up. Unfortunately, too often parents begin the Jewish upbringing of their children in a serious way only when the prospect of intermarriage threatens.

We shall address ourselves to the parents of five different age groups : the very young children, the teen-agers, the young people who are beginning to go out with non-Jewish dates, the young people who have begun to be serious about the possibility of marrying a non-Jew, and finally the young people who have decided to go ahead and marry outside the faith. Each of these categories requires a different approach; we must confess that they represent a sequence of diminishing possibilities of success. That is to say, the influence of parents on children declines as the children grow. This is, of course, natural, and in most instances desirable. What is important in this context is that parents must begin to think about the problem of intermarriage when the children are still very young. The roots of Jewish consciousness and Jewish loyalty can never be too deep.

For the Parents of the Very Young

If one were to ask, what is the major objective in the Jewish upbringing of children? We would say : *cultivating nostalgias.* It is quite apparent that the truly significant elements of Judaism as a religion and as a culture cannot be transmitted to the very young. They have no capacity — ordinarily — to grasp the profound religious and ethical implications of the Jewish tradition. The major task, therefore, should be to create the kind of atmosphere of childhood which the growing boy or girl, and later the mature young man or woman will look back upon with genuine pleasure. Jewish living must be remembered in the years that follow with joy. It must be associated with Sabbaths and festivals that appealed to the child. This means associations with sounds, sights, and tastes that spell fun, and security.

Judaism should be recalled as the reasons for getting the family together, for singing and eating, drinking and playing. These produce what might be called the "visceral" experiences, those which appeal not so much to the mind—the intellect, the reason—as to the psyche, the deep unconscious needs which are so often difficult for the individual to verbalize, and are virtually impossible for the child to articulate. These experiences, however, penetrate to the very essence of the child's personality, and account, in many instances, for the difference between a later attraction to Judaism and a rejection of it. Psychologists tell us that much of what goes for "atheism" or "agnosticism" is merely a rationalization of deep-seated antagonism to Jewish experiences associated with childhood.

This does not mean, of course, that a Jewish childhood must be a continuous holiday or party. Growing up involves discipline and study, and these are not always easy to achieve. But even these experiences must be associated in the mind of the child with love and kindness, with consistent rules and regulations, with fairness and honesty in the relations between parents and children. Rabbis and teachers, we should add, are in the same general category as the parents: symbols of authority, which the children need and want but which must at the same time be symbols of compassion and warmth. Providing attractive books, records, and pictures is essential but not sufficient; the child must be surrounded by human beings who love and are worthy of love in return. What we generally call a "Jewish education" is not enough. It is not enough for parents to turn their children over to the nearest or cheapest or least-demanding religious school and expect that they will be made into Jews. If the teachers are not sympathetic and intelligent, if the rabbi is not of the highest calibre, if the other children are not truly motivated, the "education" fails. But most important, if the parents convey—even without words—the impression that they really do not care too much about Judaism; if they intimate that they are doing what they are doing simply because it is "expected" or is the thing "to be done," you may be sure that the children's souls will "register" these impressions; and these impressions may be decisive in the years to come.

To be somewhat more specific : if the parents insist upon certain ritual observances and do not carry out those observances in their own lives; if they preach the importance of study, but are never themselves seen reading a Jewish book; if they stress the value of going to the synagogue or temple, but themselves attend only twice a year—they are planting the seeds of future cynicism.

If the children ask questions about religion, God, the Torah, the Jewish people, or any related subjects, and are not given honest answers—that is, answers which they do not truly believe in—then they are laying the groundwork for future revolt. Because children are far more perceptive than we usually give them credit for; they can detect hypocrisy long before they know the word.

It is not an exaggeration to say that antidotes to intermarriage must be applied even in the very earliest years of the child's life : at two and three. For it is then that he becomes aware of the joys of the Shabbat candles, and the *kiddush* and the *hallah*. It is then that he comes to associate Jewish events with the encompassing love of parents and family. And in the years between babyhood and adolescence, the fundamental attitudes are shaped.

For the Parents of Teenagers

If your children have been blessed with the sort of upbringing described above, it is likely that they will have developed
a sense of identification with you — and through you with the
Jewish people — which will motivate them to continue their
studies into their adolescent years. During this period they will
truly begin to appreciate the treasures of Jewish thought,
ethics, literature, and custom. Providing, of course, that they
are exposed to the right kind of teachers, and providing too
that you maintain your concern for their Jewish studies — thus
helping them to resist the distractions which they are bound to
experience from their peers, who very likely will be drifting
toward indifference — then your instructions to your children
to restrict their dating to Jewish companions will not seem to
them either prejudiced or too limiting.

A word here needs to be inserted about the whole question
of dating. During the pre-adolescent years, when sex and
marriage are still remote from the immediate interests of the
child, there need be no restrictions at all to the companionships
developed — except, of course, that the companions be decent,
clean, and law abiding. But during the years of puberty,
"dating" begins. Parents should not object to social intercourse
with non-Jewish boys and girls, provided it takes place in
groups. Couple dating, in our culture, begins quite early — and
not always to the advantage of the children themselves. But we
cannot hope to swim entirely against the tide; therefore, if
couple dating cannot be further postponed, it should be
restricted to Jewish partners. For couple dating, especially in
the middle adolescent years, is the prelude to courtship; and
if the parental objection to intermarriage is to be asserted
strongly and effectively, it must be asserted then. Naturally,
objections will be raised. Impetuous young people will at this
point put up the strongest opposition; and it is precisely at

this point that the parents must be firm. (Much of the problem of intermarriage — among other issues — grows out of the weariness of parents. If they grow tired too soon, they may spend many years regretting the fact.)

If, on the other hand, your children have not had the privilege of receiving the sort of education which we have outlined, then your problem is likely to be a more difficult one. Your adolescent children will not understand the reason for your "sudden" preoccupation with the future of Judaism. They will not understand why you should now start to make distinctions between Jews and non-Jews with respect to their differing ways of life or thought.

Nevertheless, despite the difficulty, adolescence presents parents with a "second chance." Intensive efforts must be made to compensate for the neglect or the failures of pre-adolescent training. (Incidentally, we must be prepared to take advantage of this second chance even if strenuous efforts were exerted in the early years, and the training did not for some reason "take.") This is the time to give your boys and girls every opportunity to see Judaism in action on the highest level.

This means a trip to Israel for a summer — or for at least a few weeks, with a group, under expert supervision. It means summer camps where the Jewish ingredient is stressed in an intelligent manner. It means seeing to it that the family watch television programs of high calibre which exposit the ideals of Jewish religion, or dramatize Jewish historic events in a thrilling way. It means bringing books into the home — and reading them along with the children — which portray Jewish history or personalities inspiringly. It means conducting discussions at home on topics of vital Jewish concern. It means giving of *oneself* intelligently to some phase of Jewish communal responsibility; teaching by example the mitzvah of *tzedakah*. It means encouraging the children to take courses in high school — if they are available — in Hebrew; or extra-curricular courses in Judaism at the local synagogue or temple or community center. It means taking them with you when you go to hear a lecture by some outstanding Jewish personality.

In brief, these are the years when the adolescents must be exposed to any and all Jewish influences. We must bear in mind that it is during this period that their minds begin to awaken to the culture about them. In high school they are now reading books of merit, on a mature level. They are learning history, the history of other nations, in which the Jews are rarely if ever involved.

General education has a tendency to impress young people with the small size and the allegedly small influence of Jews upon the civilization of the West. The non-Jewish curriculum does not give sufficient credit to the Jews; nor does it place Jews in a favorable light. Adolescents are strongly influenced by this kind of general education and their childhood notions of the centrality of the Jews in the world (at least in *their* world) are rudely shattered. Hence, the prime importance of counteracting these impressions by demonstrating to them that, throughout the history of western culture, Jews and Judaism have played a vital role. If they are called upon later to make a painful decision regarding intermarriage, this knowledge may become one of the factors in the decision.

However, we cannot stress too strongly that all the external influences that may be brought to bear upon the adolescent are of little avail if the relations with their parents are not satisfactory. This does not mean that we expect smooth sailing all the time. That is beyond the realm of possibility, since adolescence is the classical age for rebellion. Young people then want to start thinking of themselves as grown-up, as no longer requiring the guidance of their elders. They are beginning to feel the thrill of independence. Often they insist upon taking jobs — no matter how poorly paid — so that they can experience the satisfaction of earning their allowances.

When we speak of good relations we mean maintaining friendly channels of communication between parents and children. This sounds easier than it is, for adolescence is often the time when children stop telling their parents "everything;" just as it is the time when children stop listening to everything their parents are likely to say. Parents should expect challenge—and not seek to suppress it; nor should they ridicule these immature efforts to sound grown up. And no matter how hard it may be, parents should not panic when some of the fundamentals of Judaism are questioned—even the value of Judaism and the need for its survival.

This is the time when young people go through their atheistic period. (Indeed, one distinguished Jewish philosopher has said that no man worth his salt has not been an atheist at one time or another.) Parents should not resort to condemnation, nor disapproval of any kind; they should take the questions seriously and discuss them with their children.

Second, they should keep in mind—and convey to the youngster—that "atheism" is a philosophical problem which many people—Jews and non-Jews—have grappled with; and that it does not necessarily imply the need for, or a justification for, dissociating oneself from the Jewish people. One may change one's views without finding it necessary to change one's affiliation. Too often, young people associate Judaism solely with certain theological positions, when as a matter of fact it is a complex of culture, custom, language, literature, and history : a system of values and religion. A complete Jew makes religion the focus of his Judaism; but if for a longer or shorter period of his life he is assailed by doubts about the presence of Divinity in the cosmos, he does not cease to be—nor should he cease to be—a Jew. For as long as he remains a Jew, he may at least be sure that he will not embrace an idolatrous religion.

If parents too have their doubts and questions they should candidly admit to them, and not try to pretend that *their* faith has been constant and unwavering. If resort to books or a rabbi will be of help, nothing would please the youngster more than to appeal jointly to these authorities.

For the adolescent is now in the stage where he no longer really believes that his parents are all-knowing and all-powerful. It is therefore best for the parents to concede openly that they too are still seeking — if they are — and that questions of religious faith sometimes take a lifetime to resolve, and sometimes are never completely resolved.

But do not treat all such challenges with equal seriousness. Sometimes children express their rebellion against some form of parental authority in an oblique way. They do not come right out and say what is on their minds; perhaps sometimes they themselves are not entirely aware of what it is that troubles them. But in desperation they are likely to attack their parents in their parents' most vulnerable spot — Judaism; and they will vent their spleen on that. Frequently the very *sancta* which children hold up to ridicule or contempt at home they will defend staunchly away from home, to their friends or their teachers. Hot discussions at home are likely to be mere rehearsals for them of parallel "bull sessions" among their peers.

These are indeed the crucial years too, though they are different in character from the first period. In early childhood, verbalization counts the least. Then, clear demonstrations of love are needed; and appeals to the senses : taste, smell, sound, sight . . .In the second stage, ideals and values must be put into the setting of words. Adolescents are endless talkers — and seemingly endless arguers. For this parents must be ready : equipped with the proper attitudes and information. *They must keep open the channels of communication,* so that all questions may be thoroughly explored together. (At least, *almost* all — for children never tell all.) And most important, *parents must not get tired.*

When the Son or Daughter Begins to Date a Non-Jew

Parents set limits and hope that their children will live within them. This applies to their sex behavior, their drinking, their smoking, their spending habits—as well as to dating of non-Jewish boys or girls. What we have said about the urge to test themselves and their parents through verbal debate will now take the form of direct action. If they permit their parents to know just what they are doing, it is because they want to ascertain how far they can go, whether the limits set for them by their parents are truly fixed. Thus, going out with a non-Jew, more or less regularly, and letting the parents know that this is happening, may be their way of asking whether the parents actually have meant what they have always said about opposing intermarriage. (If the young person does not inform his parents of his frequent dating of a non-Jew, it is because he already knows the answer, and probably intends to ignore his parents' wishes. At best, he is testing himself—hoping to clarify his own feelings, without involving his parents—who, he assumes, will certainly take violent exception to his behavior.)

Parents should understand that young people frequently become infatuated with members of the opposite sex; and that these infatuations do not last. It is impossible to advise, in a generalized way, how to act in these situations. The discerning parents have to decide for themselves whether this falling in love is to be taken seriously or not. To be perfectly safe—as safe as one can be in these circumstances—the parents should express their feelings honestly, but in such a manner as not to arouse strong counter-resistance. Here too a good deal will depend upon the relations that have been built up between the parents and their children. Too great stress cannot be laid upon the vital importance of those relations.

Before long, if all goes well, the young person will have had his fill of the testing. He will know to what extent it is true that mixed couples find certain areas of conversation awkward, if not entirely taboo. They will have ascertained just how comfortable, or ill at ease, they are in the company of someone of another faith with whom they are trying to enter upon an intimate relationship designed to blossom out to more than mere friendship. They will have come to see to what extent they share the same system of values, the same interests and opinions regarding fundamental aspects of life — religion, family, money, social responsibility, etc.

One of two things will then happen : either the "infatuation" will wear off and the crisis will pass — perhaps not to be repeated — or the young people may discover that, despite their differing backgrounds, they are compatible. They may then confront their respective parents with the decision to proceed and get married.

When the Jewish Person Decides to Marry a Non-Jew

What should the parents do then? We now come to the most painful, and of course the central, issue of our time in respect to intermarriages. If parents have done all that they could, in bringing up their child, to inculcate in him love and loyalty to Judaism and the Jewish people, if they have maintained a wholesome relation with their child, if they have demonstrated by their own example their sincere concern for the perpetuation of the Jewish tradition — but if then, despite it all, their child chooses a non-Jewish partner for life, the parents must first solemnly investigate, insofar as it is possible, whether the decision which their child has taken is a *mature* decision, or whether it represents an *immature* gesture on his or her part.

By a mature decision is meant one which has grown out of

careful and deliberate evaluation of all the problems involved in an intermarriage; one which represents neither a rebellion against parents, nor a misguided notion concerning the global significance of the marriage (e.g., its contribution to the solution of inter-faith or inter-racial questions); one which grows out of a clear recognition that their common interests and values are powerful enough to transcend the obstacles to happiness which generally stand in the way of such unions.

By an immature decision, we mean, of course, the absence of these considerations.

If the decision of the couples seems to the parents (and to those trained and concerned persons, like the doctor, the psychologist, the parents of the non-Jewish party) to be an immature one, it should be strenuously opposed — not only on the ground that it involves an intermarriage, but on the broader grounds that immature decisions of this nature are bound to lead to intense personal unhappiness. You may be sure that the young couple will assume that the objections are confined to the fact that they are contemplating an intermarriage; but parents should not be deterred for this reason from seeking to prevent the marriage. In this effort they will be supported by the most liberal persons.

On the other hand, if the two young people really know what they are doing, and are acting responsibly, on a mature level, *the parents must then exert every possible effort to react in a mature manner*. This is more easily said than done, but it is necessary here to describe exactly what a mature reaction means. It means first, being concerned for the happiness of the young couple — and not for the opinions of neighbors, relatives, or business associates. Questions of social status should not enter into the consideration of this problem. What so-and-so will say about the marriage should be of little moment.

We say this because experience has again and again revealed

that parents frequently recoil at the thought of having to tell other parents—whose children have married Jews in the approved manner—that they have "failed" in the upbringing of their children. They are "ashamed" of their neighbors.

Acting maturely means not using the power of money to set up obstacles to the marriage. Withholding financial support is punitive and vindictive; it is not constructive. Acting maturely means not allowing oneself to become emotionally or physically ill—to "punish" the children for what they are doing means resisting the temptation to treat them like strangers, with whom one will have nothing to do. Your child is still your child, and as parents your love for them must be *unconditional*. This is what distinguishes parental love from all others. It is not to be proffered on condition that children make their parents happy, and withheld if children cause their parents heartache. You have brought them up. They are what they are to the greatest extent because of what *you* are. They cannot be repudiated at will.

Constructively, the parents of the Jewish partner should propose conversion to Judaism by the non-Jewish partner. Quite often, the Jewish boy or girl wants the non-Jew to convert, but hesitates to ask out of some vague notion that it is unfair to make this demand. The fact is, however, that a wholesome marriage—and family—requires that both husband and wife share the same attachment and loyalty to a community. In an intermarriage one of the partners has to surrender his or her former association. It is not more unfair for A to ask B to convert than for B to ask A to convert. And if the young person is reluctant to suggest conversion the parents can properly propose it themselves.

Naturally, it is better for the Jewish partner to urge the conversion. But if it becomes the job of the parents, care must be taken to raise the subject with *sincerity,* and wholeheartedly. We say this because, here too, experience shows that Jewish parents sometimes hold the unfortunate position that "once a Gentile, always a Gentile." As a result, they scorn the conversion as a device to "get around" the problem of intermarriage. Such an attitude is totally alien to the spirit and the letter of Jewish tradition. In historic Judaism, one who accepts the Jewish faith and fate is to be regarded as, in every sense of the term, a full-fledged and complete Jew. The proselyte adopts Abraham the Patriarch as his or her ancestor, and symbolically becomes a true descendant of the founders of the Jewish people. Thereafter no distinction is permitted in one's attitude or behavior toward the convert. Indeed, the Rabbis of old forbade Jews even to refer to the Gentile ancestry of a proselyte; they regarded this as a form of "verbal oppression."

Second-class citizenship is not tolerated among our people. Racialism, from which we have suffered for centuries, must not be allowed to degrade the status of a non-Jew who has joined the Jewish people. Mature Jewish parents, if they wish to retain the love and loyalty of their children, and to gain the respect of their son-in-law or daughter-in-law of non-Jewish origin, must therefore in all sincerity and honesty consider the possibility of conversion as a desirable and wholly acceptable procedure.

This can lead to some embarrassment if parents, who have not been particularly concerned about the Jewish education of their children, are confronted with the challenge—both by their child and "candidate" for conversion—that they, the parents, have not previously displayed the proper interest in Judaism and therefore their insistence upon conversion is not entirely defensible. In such instances, the parents must, humbly and contritely, confess that they have been remiss in their Jewish duties, and that they desire their children to live a Jewish life. No other approach, we believe, will impress the young people. Blind objection to a match on the basis of anti-

Gentile prejudice will not be accepted graciously by the young couple — nor should it.

If They Marry Without Conversion

We must now turn, with some regret, to the possibility that the young couple decide to go ahead with the marriage, without the prior conversion of the non-Jewish party. What can one say to parents when such a sad eventuality occurs? The grief that attends such an event cannot be adequately understood by anyone who has not himself or herself experienced it. Therefore, the following may sound hollow and gratuitous. But we believe that it may contain some elements of constructive advice.

You must not regard even this rejection of parental influence, and defiance of parental wishes, as final. Those who have observed a full generation of young people possess evidence to the effect that attitudes do change — especially when the young couple begin to have children. For much of what we have written here remains academic and remote to most young Jews. The realities of family life may be observed in others; or read about in books. But when they themselves begin to live those realities, changes occur in their outlook.

We have known of couples — intermarried — who decided at the beginning that each would retain membership in his and her religious group; and the children would be given the "choice" (as they put it) when they have grown to the age when they are in a position to make their own decisions. In several such instances, after the first child was born — and sometimes, a few months before the first child was expected — the non-Jewish party voluntarily came forward and proposed that she (most frequently the pregnant wife) study and prepare for conversion so that the child might be born of a Jewish mother.

This "happy ending," however, most often occurred when good relations were preserved between the Jewish parents and the couple. Despite heartbreak and sorrow, outward manifestations of goodwill and cordiality were maintained. And so long as the parents were on cordial speaking terms with the couple, the chances of a postponed conversion were kept alive.

But even more is required: The Jewish parents must continue to reflect in their own lives the religious and ethical values which they contend they wish to see preserved in their children and grandchildren. They must carry out their Jewish communal responsibilities. They must observe Sabbaths and Holidays. They must keep alive their interest in Jewish cultural life. In other words, they must convey to the young couple that their concern for Jewish creative survival was not "put on" merely to impress their children, but that they cherish a true love for Judaism — a love which they would have preferred to transmit to their own children. However, failing that, they are determined to make this concern available to the children and grandchildren of their community, because they believe in the intrinsic value of the Jewish way of life.

There is no guarantee that the example of the parents will persuade the couple. Nor is there any absolute assurance that the realities of parenthood will have the same effect. But certainly, to lose hope, to develop a cynical and bitter attitude, and to lose the love and respect of the children are greater evils.

In Conclusion

All that has been written here may seem to offer no solution to the problem of intermarriage. It should be obvious that there is no "solution." There are only approximate solutions, and some (hopefully) preventives and some ways of reacting that are better than others. We Jews entered the twentieth century, in the free nations (especially our own) in an atmosphere of desegregation. We left the "ghettos" and became part of the very fabric of the general world. Inevitably, with Jews participating in the economic, political, and cultural life of the nation, Jews and non-Jews were going to meet, and fraternize (would we have wanted it otherwise?), fall in love and want to marry.

The non-Jews whom we meet on life's way are often excellent human beings, educated, tolerant, interesting, attractive. They represent a culture which we can respect. Those of our parents and grandparents who came from the old country were surrounded by cultures which they did not respect, on the whole; for them, remaining within the fold was not quite the problem it is for our children.

For these reasons, we must think about the problem of intermarriage even when the children are very young. This is the major burden of this essay: it is never too soon to start training them in the way that we would have them go. We must plant within their souls deep roots of love for everything Jewish; but we cannot do that unless that love is implanted within our own souls.

Over and beyond all else, we must *love* our children. This may seem superfluous advice to give to Jewish parents. But it really is not superfluous — if by love is meant genuine solicitude for their welfare and happiness. Love does not consist in giving them *things,* in indulging their every whim. It does consist in acting so that the best in *us* is made available to them. We can only hope that this will elicit the best in them.

INCIDENCE OF INTERMARRIAGE IN FAMILY LOCATION SERVICE
CASES AND SOME IMPRESSIONS REGARDING THEIR RELIGIOUS
AND PSYCHOSOCIAL BACKGROUND AND FUNCTIONING

by
Solomon Z. Weiss
Assistant Director and Counsel

In response to interest in having up-to-date information as
to the incidence of intermarriage, we have reviewed closely
all regular Family Location Service cases involving intermarriage closed in 1964: a sampling of intermarriage cases
still active and the cases closed, as well as some still open, in
our Family Court Unit. Impressions of our workers about their
experience with interfaith cases were also solicited.

We have found that out of a total of 669 regular FLS cases,
both active and closed in 1964, there were 91 mixed marriage
cases, or a little over $13\frac{1}{2}$ per cent. Of a total of 398 cases,
active and closed during 1964 in our Family Court Unit, there
were 49 such cases, or nearly $12\frac{1}{2}$ per cent of intermarried
couples. The total intermarriages in all of our cases was 140
out of 1,067, a little over 13 per cent. For the period 1956–
1961, however, the overall percentage of mixed couples had
been only 9 per cent. Thus *in these cases reviewed, there has
been a 50 per cent increase in such intermarriages.*

While the Jewish, non-Jewish or half Jewish clients who
come to our attention usually present many common economic,
social, and emotional problems—such as a poor vocational
adjustment, sexual acting out, immaturity, dependency, mental
illness or disturbance, poor family relationships, relatives'
interference, some alcoholism and even some delinquent and
criminal behavior—the intermarried cases evidenced a particularly high incidence of emotional disturbance in the client,
spouse, and/or their children. Some of them had formerly

been hospitalized for a mental condition; others have manifested considerable disturbed behavior in their day-to-day life
and functioning. Our clients and their spouses usually came
from families which were themselves, at least to some degree,
socially or psychologically handicapped.

The individuals who intermarried — Jewish and non-
Jewish — seemed to come from a population that is on the
fringe of its religious, ethnic, or cultural groups. By and large,
those Jews who intermarried seemed to have had very little
religious training or cultural orientation. If they held any
commitment to the Jewish group at all, it was marginal. The
parents, too, seemed to be minimally educated in, culturally
involved, or observant of Jewish religious practices and customs. Nevertheless, these parents often objected to their son
or daughter intermarrying and in some instances only reluct-
antly consented — and found themselves blamed later by the
non-Jewish partner as interfering in-laws.

Most of our clients are women, and in most instances they
are the ones we usually see rather than the estranged or missing
husband. Available information on the non-Jewish partners
also points to a marginal religious or cultural commitment to
the group from which they derive. Also commonly reported
by persons intermarrying were poor child–parent relationships.

In some instances, the Jewish woman had intermarried
because she had seen herself as an inadequate individual, not
having any real opportunity to marry a Jewish man, either
because of her socially unacceptable background, poor looks,
or physical condition. These women saw the prospective Jewish
partners as more deliberate in their choices — and more critical.
Some also seemed to see the Gentile boy as "more fun to be
with," a more persistent courtier, and a better spender
on dates.

To some of these Jewish men, the non-Jewish woman seemed
to be more feminine and subservient. These men tended to

see Jewish women as threatening and controlling. Others saw Jewish girls as a reminder of their mothers, which seemed to arouse a sense of guilt or anxiety in relation to sexual activity. They indicated that they felt more comfortable and uninhibited sexually with a non-Jewish woman. In some situations, self-hate seemed to play a role in the intermarriage; to others, intermarriage was a way of proving that they were more Americanized, liberal, emancipated, etc.

A close look at the day-to-day life of the intermarried couples revealed that the religious faith and obligations of the respective partners played a very minor role, and whatever religious practices were observed were on a superficial level —eventually tending to alienate the children, even when they nominally considered themselves Jewish.

While some of the couples that were seen tended to deny religious differences as an immediate causative factor of their marital conflicts, they more readily acknowledged that cultural differences, habits, and differences in values had played an important role in their incompatibility. Some when closely questioned would admit being called a "damned Jew" during heated arguments with their gentile spouses. Interference by relatives was quite a frequent complaint by one or both spouses. While complaints about in-laws are not unusual, even where both partners are Jewish, intermarriage situations often displayed pronouncedly poorer in-law relationships. Some Jewish spouses tended to look with disdain upon the living habits and ways of living of the Christian in-laws, such as alcoholism, shabby living quarters, lack of responsibility, etc. The most prevalent complaint made by the non-Jewish husband was that his Jewish in-laws were too clannish and tended to control the wife.

Most of the couples had intermarried in a civil ceremony only, but their children were usually designated or reared in the faith of their mother. The religious commitment was primarily expressed through baptism, circumcision, or being named in a synagogue. Usually there was little educational follow-up and practice in the particular religious faith. The older intermarried couples' adult children were often married to non-Jewish husbands or wives.

In a few instances, there had been conversions to the Jewish faith, but these were mostly nominal and superficial, with little observance by either spouse; when difficulties developed, the convert sometimes reverted to his or her original faith.

Although the cases reviewed were not always clear-cut as to the degree to which intermarriage created the marital conflicts—and in many instances it seemed that personality and contributing social factors were at least the primary cause for the domestic difficulties—our cases did indicate that differences in religion, cultural, or ethnic backgrounds did play a significant role, and pointed to poor prognosis for a successful reconciliation. In some instances, the role of the so-called interfering parent was quite obvious. Quite often this interference was not only in terms of religious practices but in other areas of family living.

There are a number of questions, by no means exhaustive, which may be helpful in relating ourselves to the primary question as to what should be the function and role of a Jewish Federation family agency with regard to the problem of increasing intermarriage by Jews. The following are merely suggestions:

Is intermarriage a personal matter rather than one of Jewish communal concern, and therefore to be dealt with by the Jewish family agency like other personal problems presented by Jewish clients?

Is it a responsibility of the Jewish family agency to declare a positive Jewish commitment, in relation to the phenomenon of increasing intermarriage, in order to stem the increasing tide of mixed marriages?

Does the Jewish family agency fully discharge its responsibilities by providing services to Jewish clients whatever their problems? Those arising out of intermarriage are one of the many multiple problems presented by the Jewish family in trouble.

Some feel that intermarriage is objectionable not only because it is a source of unhappiness to some families, but because it tends to promote the gradual dissolution, or at least the significant decrease, of Jewish life and the size of the Jewish community itself. Should the Jewish community take a neutral stand in spite of this?

Some people may question the basic assumption that the continuance of the Jewish community and group is jeopardized by increasing intermarriage, but in response to those who do see in the increasing intermarriage a dangerous signal of eventual assimilation, does the Jewish family agency have specific responsibility in helping to prevent such intermarriages, or to minimize their effects upon the Jewish community when intermarriage has already taken place?

One of the basic assumptions of the *family agency generally* is that its function is the preservation of *family life*. Is it the function of the Jewish family agency to preserve the integrity of the *Jewish family* and, in effect, at least the continuation of the Jewish community?

The service professions have certain values which they actually promote in the course of their practice. Is it the responsibility of the Jewish professional to promote Jewish values? Is prevention and discouragement of intermarriage one of these values?

Even though professionals and lay leaders may differ in answers to the above questions, if a significant section of the Jewish community is concerned about the dangers to Jewish continuation, is it the responsibility of the Jewish family agency to honor that concern with positive action or should it take a neutral stand? Is such neutral position really neutral in effect? These questions do seem relevant in formulating policies by and for the Jewish family agency.

INTERRACIAL JEWISH CHILDREN

by
Werner J. Cahnman

On December 2, 1959, when I was teaching at Yeshiva University, I addressed myself to a leading Orthodox rabbi in New York City with regard to the problem of interracial Jewish children. I drew his attention to a report published in the *New York Times* of October 11, 1959, bearing the headline: "Religious Rule on Adoption Bars Many Couples in State." It was reported there that the placing by adoption agencies of Negro children outside their designated religion was "standard practice in cases where the designation was Jewish" and that in six years (1953–59) about 150 children who were considered Jewish had been placed in non-Jewish homes. An apparent minority of these children were so-called "rotational" children, but the majority were children born out of wedlock to a Jewish woman and a Negro man. In the following discussion I shall refer only to the latter category.

In my letter of December 2, 1959, I said: "I believe that [the above quoted fact] constitutes a serious communal concern. To exclude children of Jewish mothers from the Jewish community is entirely against Jewish law and custom. Conduct of this sort has never been condoned in Jewish history and to condone it in the wealthiest Jewish community in existence now should be considered a matter of shame. Moreover, it appears to be a surrender to racialism and hence doubly contrary to Jewish precepts. And as it will be noted by the Negro community, it cannot fail to make our repeated confessions of liberalism in race relations sound exceedingly hollow."

On December 13, 1959, my letter was forwarded by my rabbinical friend to the Rabbinical Council of America "for action by a special RCA Committee. . . . perhaps in conjunction with certain Jewish social agencies." The Rabbinical Council was asked to contact me in the event that further steps were contemplated. I have never heard, either directly or indirectly, from any Rabbinical Council of America Committee or Rabbinical Council of America rabbi in the meantime.

However, the matter was taken up by the Committee on Child Guidance and Welfare of Federation. In the Inter-Office Memo of the Committee, dated May 26, 1960, six points of concern to the Committee were outlined, of which point three dealt with the problems of the interracial or black Jewish child. By the spring of 1963, after thorough discussion, the Committee had reached the decision to conduct an inquiry into the entire matter of the needs of these children, so that the facts and figures upon which future decisions in this area would have to be based could be made available. I was requested to submit the outline for a suitable questionnaire, and soon thereafter the Federation was asked to provide financial support. At this point, the matter got stuck again.

As a consequence of the failure to provide adequate data in time, we do not know the number of children in the black Jewish communities and we do not know the number of interracial Jewish children, both those born out of wedlock and those born to racially intermarried couples who are either legitimately Jewish or whose parents wish to have them brought up in the Jewish faith. Subsequently, I am referring to the latter two categories. In both instances the known facts are scanty, but the underlying phenomena are clear enough to enable us to formulate a number of questions which are relevant to our concern today.

Unfortunately, figures recently made known by the Louise Wise Adoption Services throw several categories of interracial children together. As far as I can ascertain from newspaper notices, among the cases processed by the Louise Wise Services there are three major categories : (1) American Indian children who are up for adoption; (2) "rotational" children who are designated as Jewish; and (3) illegitimate children of Jewish mothers and Negro fathers. The total number of these children known to Louise Wise Services during the period 1953–1963 seems to be in excess of 300 and in the absence of a reliable breakdown I will assume that the number of them who belong to the third category (the one that is of principal interest to us here) is somewhere between 200 and 250 children. What is more important is that it can be safely predicted that this number will be increasing steadily in the decades of the 60's and 70's.

I cannot speak for the Louise Wise Services, but it seems that their policy with regard to these children has been undergoing a change. In the past, the idea seems to have prevailed that the "needs" of the colored child are best served by its placement in a colored home, but two stubborn facts have militated against inflexibility in this regard : (1) There are many more Negro children in need of adoption than there are Negro homes both suitable and ready to receive them; and (2) The desirability of integration directs the search away from Negro homes for colored children and towards white homes — if the latter can be made available.

As a result, the Louise Wise Services has issued an appeal to white couples who are willing to adopt colored children to come forward. This appeal has failed thus far. But I note that the appeal has been made to the white community in general, not specifically to the Jewish segment of this community, and

I conclude from this observation that the Louise Wise Services might welcome a special effort by the Jewish community to come to their aid in this regard. I do not know of any better place to start than the Commission on Synagogue Relations of Federation.[1]

[1] Editor's Note: Florence G. Brown, Executive Director of Louise Wise Services explains, in shedding light on Dr. Cahnman's statement:

We have placed over 350 children of interracial background. The figure for the ten years, from 1953 to 1963, was approximately 300 and, as indicated by Dr. Cahnman, the largest number in this group were children born to Jewish mothers and Negro fathers. I believe we would find that in the ten year period close to 250 out of the 300 were in this group. I would also agree that the number has been increasing.

Dr. Cahnman's statement that there are many more Negro children in need of adoptive homes than there are Negro homes suitable and ready to receive them is correct. However, we also believe that there are many more Negro families who could be found for the children needing adoption and that the agencies all need to do much more in recruiting these families. Our efforts in encouraging white families to adopt part Negro children is not to be interpreted as an effort in lieu of reaching Negro families. On the contrary, the greater emphasis still needs to be in reaching more Negro families. We do believe, however, that the approach should be a broader one and that, in addition to the fact that there are not enough Negro families for the children, it is in the interests of the children themselves to have a wider selection of families. It is important to note that when a child who is part white and part Negro is placed for adoption, whether he is placed with a Negro family or a white family, this is a transracial placement. I mention this because there seems to be an assumption that we are crossing racial lines only if the child is placed with a white family. For children who are of two races the best selection of the home that is right for the individual child can be made by recruitment of Negro families, white families and interracial families.

Dr. Cahnman is correct in his statement that our appeal has been to the white community in general and not specifically to the Jewish community. We certainly do welcome a special effort by the Jewish community and I would hope that in the future more Jewish families will express an interest in adoption of Jewish children who are partially of another race.

I should like to note that I have some question about Dr. Cahnman's statement about integration. One could interpret from this statement that the whole purpose of our efforts in recruiting more white families is because of the integration movement. This is not correct. Our main purpose is that of meeting the needs of the children under our care and we are not interested in using our children as a means of fighting a cause. It is undoubtedly true that the civil rights movement and the general

However, the problem is much wider in scope. There can be no doubt that the number of interracial marriages in this country is increasing. According to a study by David M. Heer of the School of Public Health, Harvard University, the percentage of Negro males marrying white females has risen in recent years from 3.36 to 3.96 in California, from 9.09 to 17.78 in Hawaii, and from 1.09 to 1.90 in Michigan; the figure for New York is likely to be of about the same order of magnitude as the figure for California. With the rise of the Negro middle classes these figures *must* rise in the future. Now, the point of interest here is that the percentage of Jewish females in these liaisons is undoubtedly high now and should be presumed to stay high in the future. I base this judgment on two studies: (1) a study by Joseph Golden on "The Negro-White Intermarried in Philadelphia" (*American Sociological Review, April 1953*), and (2) a doctoral dissertation by Charles E. Smith, as reported in the *New York Times* of October 18, 1963. According to the Golden study, of 44 white brides of Negro grooms in Philadelphia, 19 — that is 43 per cent — were Jewish; according to the Smith study, out of 22 couples analyzed 11 — that is 50 per cent — consisted of Protestant Negro grooms and Jewish spouses. Since the Smith study is not meant to be statistically representative, it may be assumed that between 60 per cent and 70 per cent of all white spouses of Negro men in the New York Metropolitan area are of Jewish derivation.

It would require a separate study to inquire into the reasons for the (presumably) high participation of Jewish females in legitimate as well as illegitimate liaisons with Negro males, but one cannot exclude the factor of revolt against prevailing

feeling with regard to integration may make transracial placements more possible at this time than was true in the past. Although Dr. Cahnman states that our "appeal has failed thus far," this is not correct. Although we cannot speak of many placements of interracial children with white families, the number is gradually increasing.

values in the family and in society. And why, one might further ask, do Jewish young women participate in this revolt in such a disproportionate way? It is because they are more sensitive to injustice? Is it because they are insecure in their Jewish attachments and hence inclined to register their protest against society in an area not specifically designated as "Jewish" rather than in an area so designated? Or is it because stuffy and prejudicial attitudes are especially conspicuous in the Jewish middle classes? Even if one assumes that all of these motivational factors are present to an equivalent degree, the conclusion seems inescapable that prejudicial attitudes in the field of race relations will not only prevent us from doing our duty by those of our brothers and sisters whose skin is colored, but that they will also tend to alienate increasing numbers of young Jews from their Jewish allegiance. Therefore, no matter how one looks at it, the problems of the interracial Jewish couples, the interracial Jewish children, and the children in the black Jewish communities are both interrelated and of strategic importance among the problems of Jewish concern at this time. One must therefore express the hope that Jewish Federations and social agencies will act accordingly.

4

Judaism and Philanthropy

A notable paper on Tzedakah has become an annual tradition of the Commission on Synagogue Relations. This is as it should be, because the ideas and ideals of Tzedakah are the lifeblood which sustains and supplies the vital force to the communal body that is crucial to positive Jewish existence.

The Commission is now grappling with the "re-examination of the role, the methods, and the raison d'être of Jewish Philanthropy." There is a compelling need for a meaningful, fructifying philosophy of Jewish Philanthropy in today's America. At its core is the very survival of the community itself and the dedicated commitment of its members in a united front encompassing all communal groups, in order to ensure Jewish continuity.

To this end, Rabbi Sandrow's paper, with its analysis of "The Meaning of Tzedakah for the Modern Jew," takes its place alongside the previous excellent essays on Tzedakah in the Commission's history.

161

Dr. Twersky's essay is a profound exposition on three questions: (1) What are the ideological roots of charity? (2) What are the quantitative and qualitative demands that charity makes on the individual? (3) Is charity a particular performance of the Jew as a universal expression of the dignity of man?

THE MEANING OF TZEDAKAH FOR THE MODERN JEW

by
Rabbi Edward T. Sandrow

Love of fellow man, care of young and old, the sick, the underprivileged, the lonely, the disturbed, the frightened—all these stem from the basic message of the Torah, the substructure and keystone of our Faith. The Talmud (Sotah 14a) makes it abundantly clear that "The Torah begins and ends with deeds of beneficence, of human kindness."

We are as human beings and, as Americans, concerned about the social needs of *all* human beings. The question then arises: why must we develop and support specific *Jewish* philanthropic institutions? Can we not find outlets for our social philosophy in community service organizations of a non-denominational character? Why is it then that we have Jewish Federations in every major Jewish community? Why do we establish and support agencies within Federations which cater primarily to Jews, to Jewish needs, to the Jewish community? The Jewish communities from the days of ancient Babylonia to the modern world provided social institutions for our brethren who required them. It is because there is rooted in our tradition the desire to heal our own, in *addition* to the *love* and *care* we show to *any* human being created in the image of God. There is also an intangible drive or a conscious-

ness on the part of Jews to feel more at home when they seek
out the institutions which bear the imprimatur of Judaism
or the Jewish spirit or what we call a sense of Jewish peoplehood. The whole subject has fascinated me. And, in searching
the writings of social psychologists and social workers there is
no established scientific reason as to why Jews seek out Jewish
agencies. May I present a non-scientific proposition. It is
because there is a will to identify with the Jewish group even
on the part of those who have wandered away from the totality
of Jewish life or Jewish culture. Even those of our people who
have become quasi-assimilated, who have shed the honorable
garment of Jewish religious practice, and who are ignorant
of the historical process which has made us a people rooted in
a religious tradition, still support and take pride in Jewish
welfare agencies. Not only is philanthropy the sole contact they
have with their people, but they prefer a Jewish family service
agency when domestic problems beset them, or an old age
home conducted under Jewish auspices whenever they have
need of such a welfare agency. When a Jew stops either giving
to Federation or using Jewish social service facilities, you can
be sure he has practically disengaged himself from our people.

More than that! Social service for the Jew is wrapped up
with the Jewish religion and that is why Federation is wise in
seeking out the congregations as a never-drying reservoir of
support. To the Jew, religion never divorced itself from the
education, the healing, the moral dimension which is so vital
in interpersonal relations. When someone mentions "Federation" to me, it is not statistics which reifies it for me. Federation
conjures up in my mind a vital instrument in the historical
and spiritual continuity of our people. For millennia the Jew
has had his rituals and customs — his Sabbaths and his festivals.
Behind all these rituals were not just *blind* and *mechanical*
practice. There was always social purpose and moral idealism.
When the Jew prepared for the Sabbath even in the midst of

poverty, he set aside a crumb of bread to share with one less
fortunate. When the Jewish housewife lit her Sabbath candles,
she made sure that a coin, no matter how small, had already
been placed in the *Tzedakah* box. When the Jew began his
Seder on Passover night he called out, "Let those who are
hungry come in and eat with us." When the Jew kept and
keeps the dietary laws he senses in them a divine commandment to respect and cherish living things to avoid torture and
pain to a lower animal. The pages of our literature are
replete with ethical principles which are the substructure of
Judaism from which flows *Tzedakah*—of which "Federation"
is a symbol.

The overriding principle of Judaism is that "the earth is the
Lord's and the fulness thereof" and that man is "a partner
with God" in this world. Judaism stresses the thought that if
we are all children of God then all men are brothers. When the
Bible speaks of the needy person, or one who is reduced to
poverty, he is called "brother." We have such powerful
examples in the Torah, "If thy *brother* be waxen poor" . . .
"Let thy *brother* live with thee" . . . "Shut not thy hand from
thy *brother*?" . . . "Open thine hand to thy needy *brother*" . . .
etc. etc. The rabbis in the Talmud were not content merely to
the giving of a dole, a handout. Even in their time this was
old-fashioned, lady-bountiful charity. They felt that people
had to be given reassurance and love and be spoken to with
kindness, much like the basic intent of today's case worker.
They said, "He who gives a 'prutah' [a copper coin] to the
poor man is blessed with six blessings, but he who encourages
him with *kind* words is blessed with eleven blessings." The
sages were quick to point out that the Psalmist writes "Happy
is he who *considers* the poor" and not "Happy is he who gives
to the poor."

You must have heard the following fact on many occasions :
There is no Jewish word for charity. Jewish philanthropy

became synonymous with *Tzedakah* on "the practice of righteousness." It embraced the term *Gemilat Hasadim* or "the bestowing of kindness." And both terms became an integral part of the Jewish way of life.

Not only prayer and study were rooted in the synagogue but also *Tzedakah*. Up until comparatively recent times, the *offices* of the Jewish welfare agencies were in the synagogue —in Babylonia, in Spain, in Germany, in Eastern Europe. The Codes of Maimonides (twelfth century), of Jacob ben Asher (fourteenth century), of Joseph Caro (sixteenth century), aside from pointing up this fact, all set forth high and lofty conceptions regarding the relation of the Jewish religion and *Tzedakah,* and their common roots in the *synagogue* and its goals. Read their legal maxims : They never said "Poverty is good," or that the poor must "always be with us." They referred to a Talmudic saying that "the guiding spirit of poverty is called *Nobal,*"a term which means "dirt"or"human degradation." They cried out against the mortification of the flesh. They—the prophets of the Bible, the rabbis of the Talmud, the scholarly giants of the Middle Ages—thundered against the loss of human independence and self respect.

Can we not see, therefore, how ingrained in us there is this will to *maintain* Jewish agencies and, on the other hand, why Jews have to this day sought out Jewish agencies for social services. Even if a Jew is not religious in the formal sense he cannot draw a line of demarcation between the *Kodesh* and *Hol,* between the spiritual component of *Tzedakah* and the act of giving. *Tzedakah* is religion ! What I have been leading up to is an undoubted opinion that no matter what new ideas are made part of the whole science of social work—no matter what new psychiatric and socio-psychiatric methods are used in treating the disturbed and mentally ill, what new theories are developed in the science of geriatrics, or in the handling of juvenile delinquents—there remains a deep-rooted, indestructible spiritual component in our work. When we help educate a Jewish child in the Torah and in Judaism, we are developing an ethically sensitive Jew and a *future giver* to Federation. When we reconstruct human lives that are in the midst of anguish of soul—when a social worker salvages a family and helps it solve some of its problems, when our emotionally ill are rehabilitated through our hospitals and convalescent homes and know that the pattern stems from the Judaism of the Torah and the synagogue, the Judaism which speaks of God and the dignity of man—we know also that Federation's agencies are symbols of the way the Jew has always *sanctified* human life.

Do you get, then, a glimpse of the meaning of *Tzedakah* for the modern Jew? I was tremendously impressed with an address delivered by the Honorable Abraham Ribicoff before the 30th General Assembly of the Council of Jewish Federations and Welfare Funds. He called for "new ideas and new solutions." He showed how our society is more complicated today than it ever was. He indicated how "even poverty is different." He called for positive goals—"to move people off relief . . . by renewing their spirit and creating economic and social opportunities for them." He urged that our society stress "the integrity and preservation of the family unit." Then proudly he said to Federations, "You have *proved* your concern for your fellow human beings and your ability to *translate this concern* into constructive action." He was using the terms of a spiritually minded governmental leader rooted in our tradition and he reinterpreted them for our time. When Mr. Ribicoff speaks about the need for the individual to become "self helping," he is using the language of the modern social worker clothed in the spirit of basic Jewish morality.

As to the social worker—like the teacher a dedicated and consecrated servant of the community—she has my deep respect. She must listen sensitively and respond spontaneously.

She must, as Paul Tillich puts it, carry out the principle of "listening, responding, transforming love." She must help the individual find himself to the point where "he can consider himself as necessary." This makes the social worker also a partner of the Almighty. The social worker is then carrying out the Jewish concept of *Tzedakah*. She is giving man a spiritual lift, helping him find life worthwhile.

The spirit of *Tzedakah* is in the blood of the modern Jew. When you give to Federation you are identifying with a 4,000-year-old way of life. You cannot *trace* all your ancestors but you can be sure that in every age and in every clime your ancestors *practiced Tzedakah*. There burned in them a passion for loving kindness. That is your tradition and mine. Our own America is an heir to that spiritual and democratic tradition. We live in the most affluent and prosperous country of history. No Jew can, then, in this combination of circumstance be indifferent to that great inheritance of *Tzedakah* which is so deeply rooted in our hearts.

Tzedakah is a gadfly to conscience. It is therefore a highly ethical ideal. Shakespeare says in *Hamlet* that "Conscience doth make cowards of us all." Justice Horace Stern of Philadelphia once said that he feels quite the reverse. He said, "conscience makes *heroes* of us all." What did he mean? He implied that *Tzedakah* as a spur to conscience is part of our "sense of duty." It is the "still small voice" which builds character, which leads to duty — duty to God and man. What a man practices in the way of *Tzedakah* is a reflection of his thinking and feeling. The person who is sympathetic and generous has a glow inside him. My father, of blessed memory, used to speak of the Jew who went out of his way to do *Tzedakah* as a "schoener mensch," an "attractive personality." You grow a soul, and just as physical exercise strengthens your muscles and sends the blood coursing through your veins, so your soul expands when the moral blood circulates.

When a man practices *Tzedakah* he sets an example for others. Every one of us influences others. In that sense we are *all* leaders. And a leader is a person who espouses a cause with enthusiasm. It is true in our homes and in our businesses. It should be true in our communities, in our synagogues, in our Federation commitment. This is a tremendous challenge : *Tzedakah* is catching ! Every dollar we give brings more dollars from others. The influence we wield on others gives us all a double responsibility. We enrich others as we give of ourselves.

Lastly, *Tzedakah* is a symbol that life has purpose — that there is a God who is involved in man's development. We live in a very uncertain time : There are threats and counter-threats to peace, there is a cold war and a power struggle between nations, there are people who live in fear and insecurity, economic systems are in flux. When we carry out the basic tenets of our religious tradition and say with the Psalmist as the Jew did in all ages, in times of joy and of tragedy, "I will not die but live and declare the works of the Eternal," the Jew reemphasized his faith in the *worthwhileness* of life. *Tzedakah* gave him a sense of communion with the past. It made him accountable. It made him develop sensitivity to God's creatures. It gave him a sense of destiny. In the very act of *Tzedakah* we pledge our loyalty to the democratic ideals of America, because we say that all creatures are made in the divine image and that our task until man's inhumanity to man ceases is to help and to love our fellowmen.

All this if threaded through would be part of a single design — the pattern of Judaism colored and beautified by its hand-maiden *Tzedakah*. Let each one of us as an individual make this mental summary: "The meaning of *Tzedakah* for the modern Jew has its roots in the Jewish religion and in our sense of peoplehood. It stems from Torah and Talmud, from prophet and sage. It is ancient and yet modern; it makes me more human; it enriches my conscience; it develops my character;

it makes me a leader. It is my way of symbolizing the worth-whileness of life and the reality of God." Professor Heschel said it another way at the White House Conference on Aging. If I may paraphrase him : *Tzedakah* is an aid to fulfillment. It is part of religion which binds man to creation and to the Creator and enables him to face the future with hope. *Tzedakah* is the call to Jewish hearts and willing spirits to be grateful for the blessings of life and to embrace all men generously ! It is the ferment of the Jewish spirit. We must never let it disintegrate or die. This will be our task for many generations to come.

PHILANTHROPY AND THE SYNAGOGUE

by
Rabbi Isaac N. Trainin
Director, Commission on Synagogue Relations

Every drama must have a theme. The drama we enact the last Monday of each April has as its theme, *Tzedakah*.

Tzedakah, what an elusive, exotic, multi-faceted, and chameleon-like word. Righteousness, justice, and equity — and yet *Tzedakah* means much more. To fully understand it one has to live it in truth.

How different our concept is from its equivalent in other languages. In Latin the word *caritas* means benevolence and help that is extended to the poor and the needy. The English word "charity," derived from the Latin, suggests the image of one in a fortunate position conferring largesse upon one less fortunate. In its wider implication, it connotes the exercise of superior virtue by an individual.

"Philanthropy," coming from the Greek word *love for mankind,* is the spirit of goodwill toward one's fellow men. But it is too impersonal. The Greeks equated philanthropy with harmony. In our faith *Tzedakah* is akin to holiness. The Prophet Isaiah declares, הָאֵל הַקָּדוֹשׁ נִקְדַּשׁ בִּצְדָקָה "The Holy God is sanctified by justice." *Tzedakah* to us implies a categorical imperative. We recognize no distinction between the giver and the beneficiary — both are born equal. The manner of giving charity is as important as the act of giving.

The Psalms tells us: "Defend the poor and fatherless, do justice to the afflicted and needy." It does not say: "Have pity," but rather "do justice." We Jews do not have pity, we do not give charity or alms, we do justice.

Even the Torah depends upon justice. Therefore, said Rabbi Elazar, "Immediately after the Ten Commandments come the enactments about justice" (Exodus XXI), about man's responsibility to his neighbor. Lofty moral principles are the foundation of our faith — The duties of man to God, the duties of man toward man. But no sooner were the Ten Commandments received on Mt. Sinai when Moses related them to *Tzedakah* — to the practical applications of the Ten Commandments to a just society. Laws are meaningless, unless practiced and applied to all men — at all times. Justice, whether to your profit or loss, whether in word or in action, whether to Jew or non-Jew, so said Bachya ben Asher.

Tzedakah, and its co-principle, Gemileth Chasadim, acts of loving kindness, constitute one of the three pillars of Judaism which a Jewish community is exhorted to promote — along with the Torah; that is, knowledge and observance of Jewish law and Avodah. Gemileth Chasadim is not only a private duty but the collective responsibility of a community. Support of the poor, the wayfarer, the sick, the aged, the widow, and the orphan belong under this category. It is true that an isolated Jew can still be a Jew without a community. Nevertheless, Judaism attains its consummation only in and through communal life — through the synagogue, religious schools, and philanthropic organizations.

And although our rabbis generally agree that of the three
pillars of Judaism, the study of the Torah is the most essential
to the continuity of our civilization, the basic purpose of Torah
is to teach us to live by *Tzedakah* — justice and righteousness.
This concept is as old as the Jewish people. When the Bible
tells us of the attributes of Noah which made him worthy of
being saved at the time of the flood, it merely describes him
as a *Tzadik*. We are not given his genealogy nor his accom-
plishments, but are merely told that he led a life of righteousness. When Abraham pleads with the Almighty to spare the
city of Sodom, it is on the basis that maybe there will be
enough *Tzadikim* to make the city worthy of being saved.
Abraham was not concerned with the city's art, music,
literature, or refinements. These qualities, as worthy as they
are by themselves, do not justify calling a civilization just or
meritorious. Indeed, legend itself speaks of the 36 *Tzadikim*
for whose sake the world exists.

The patriarch Jacob established the concept of Tithe for
all time and for Jews everywhere. Throughout the ages, the
conscientious Jew kept a scrupulous account of his yearly
earnings. A tenth part of it went to philanthropy. He put aside
this tenth from his property and thenceforth considered himself only as its distributor. So you can see the idea of a charitable foundation, so popular today, has its roots in ancient
times. The Jew considered himself the fiduciary and this Tithe
(*maaser*) was his responsibility. In other words, he gave to
suffering humanity what, in any case, already belonged to it.
Tzedakah is constantly on the lips of a Jew. When a child is
named, we offer *Tzedakah*. Every *simcha* is hallowed by
offering *Tzedakah*. When a Jew departs his earthly abode,
Tzedakah is offered for his soul.

Each Sabbath we recite a beautiful prayer in the synagogue.
Its roots are in antiquity. We say : "And all those who occupy

themselves in faithfulness, in communal affairs, may the Holy One, blessed be He, give them their due reward."

Thus, we take cognizance on each Sabbath of the three cardinal principles of Judaism—of the Torah and worship as the proper functions of the synagogue and Gemileth Chasadim, which, while carried out through the instrumentality of philanthropic organizations, nevertheless combine with the Torah and Avodah in spelling out and delineating the duties and responsibilities of the Jew.

For we maintain that, as a man is not well unless all his organs are functioning properly, a Jew by classic definition is one who pays allegiance to and who upholds these three eternal pillars of Judaism. Otherwise we "compartmentalize" our faith; one practices *Tzedakah*, another concerns himself only with the synagogue, and a third devotes himself exclusively to the study of the Torah.

Not every Jew can be a great philanthropist—not every Jew can be a scholar. But all Jews can adhere to and support and encourage these three principles of Judaism. It is true, however sad, that today we hear more and more talk about adjective Judaism. But for the sincere Jew there is no room for such distinctions. We affirm that *Tzedakah* is an indivisible principle—for there is no adjective *Tzedakah*. It is one: for all Jews, for all men, for all times.

The purpose of a Commission on Synagogue Relations is to strengthen the link between the synagogue and philanthropy. Consisting of synagogue laymen, rabbis, social workers, and representatives of philanthropic institutions associated with Federation, our philosophy, program, and aims are to encourage the Jewish community to drink from the eternal well of the synagogue and to wear proudly the simple unadorned clothing of *Tzedakah*. Thus, our functions are clearly defined: (a) *To create a communal leadership whose roots are both in the synagogue and in philanthropy;* (b) *To accentuate the Jewish elements of philanthropy.*

It should not be forgotten, it must not be forgotten, that Jewish charity is basically a religious duty. As such it cannot be divorced from the sum total of Jewish life. We believe that Jewish social workers must possess a knowledge of Jewish history and tradition. They cannot isolate themselves from Jewish thinking and expect to fulfill their functions adequately. Philanthropy must constantly guard the quality of Jewish services so that, for the benefit of the total Jewish community, we can forge a symphony of Judaism consisting of Torah, Avodah, and Gemileth Chasadim; instead of a cacophony of diverse and strident elements which are part of the Jewish organism and yet not totally belonging to it.

And the synagogue Jew must realize his responsibility to the total community and to philanthropy. It is sad that so many Jews who are active in synagogue life stand apart and look on with neutrality at the philanthropic endeavors of their community. It is inconsistent that there should be a lack of correlation between devotion to the synagogue and philanthropic concern and generosity.

It is, therefore, the duty of religious leadership, both lay and rabbinic, to encourage synagogue members to participate in the philanthropic community. *Tzedakah* cannot be theoretical. It must be practiced. Parenthetically, may I point out that in the building of the Tabernacle Moses was exhorted by the Almighty in the following words:

"Speak unto the children of Israel, that they take for ME an offering; of every man whose heart maketh him willing ye shall take an offering." In other words, here was the beginning of voluntary philanthropy. On the other hand, when it comes to *Tzedakah,* there was, as I stated before, a categorical imperative both for the individual and the community.

Now I know the sacrifice made by synagogue leadership in

erecting and maintaining houses of worship and schools of study; and how easily one can say, "my responsibility ends there." But all of us in the community use communal philanthropic institutions and, therefore, as synagogue leadership, we indeed carry the heavy burden of wearing the triple crown of Judaism which, while sacred, is heavy and costly.

On the other hand, we must encourage the philanthropic Jew, no matter how noble his devotion to *Tzedakah* is, to become part of the synagogue world and to participate in the overall responsibilities of the religious life of his community, for if Judaism is not a religion — it is nothing.

On a more practical level the Commission is involved in programs of joint interest to the synagogue and Federation. I refer to Transients and Indigents, the Aftercare Programs, Divorce and Separation, the Black Jew, the cooperation between the rabbi and the Jewish social worker, the project on mental health and Judaism — involving a dialogue between psychiatrists and rabbis; also, the attempt to correlate medical practice in Jewish tradition, which has resulted in a pamphlet issued under the name "Hospital Compendium," the first of its kind in American Jewish history. In short, the building of a solid bridge between the synagogue and philanthropy.

It is difficult to evaluate our success in this two-fold undertaking. All of us tend to exaggerate our successes and rationalize our failures. Our successes we credit to our genius, our failures to obstruction and lack of cooperation on the part of others. But I hope we have an open end, and approach it with open hearts and open minds.

There is a great deal of concern today about the vanishing Jew and about the survival of the Jewish civilization. Take away the synagogue, remove yourself from Jewish philanthropy, and you will have destroyed the great pillars which are the quintessence of our faith. For those who don't care — and oh how we wish everyone cared — there is no problem; for us who do, the task, although difficult, is clear.

A story is told of a rabbi who had been desperately trying to reach a rich Jew to speak to him about a contribution to the rabbi's institution but he could not reach him over the phone. He finally got to his secretary and said to tell Mr. X that a mutual relative died and left a large legacy which the rabbi would like to discuss with Mr. X. You can be sure that Mr. X called the rabbi back promptly and asked him who had died and what was the size of the legacy. The rabbi replied, "our great teacher Moses died and he left you and me the Torah which is our mutual concern." Friends, the future of Judaism in general and *Tzedakah* in particular are our mutual concerns.

To summarize: the Commission is a dialogue between philanthropy and the synagogue. Our unflinching loyalty and devotion to *both* is needed to assure a flourishing future for our people and for our way of life. Apart, the prospects are bleak: The concept — or myth, if you will — that philanthropy belongs in the realm of the secular, that religion belongs only in the synagogue, and that both move in never-meeting parallel lines is a contradiction in terms and alien to Jewish experience.

This is the task. What a challenge — but what an opportunity! We fervently hope that the house of worship (the synagogue) and the house of *Tzedakah* will be equal to this unending task. We may conclude with these words (בארח צדקה חיים) "In the path of *Tzedakah*, righteousness, there is life." This then is our theme. This is our goal. Let us together strive for it.

The author acknowledges the following sources:
(1) Former Chief Rabbi of Israel, Rabbi J. H. Hertz.
(2) "What It Means To Be A Jew": Rabbi Charles E. Shulman.

(3) *Essays* by Rabbi S. R. Hirsch.

(4) Various passages from the Pentateuch, Prophets, Talmud, and Hassidic sources.

THE JEWISH ATTITUDE TOWARDS THE WELFARE STATE

by
Dr. Isadore Twersky,
Harvard University

The treatment of this theme is beset with "occupational" or topical hazards; it can imperceptibly pass from the carefully lined notebook of the historian or analyst to the supple and suggestive text of the preacher or partisan. Welfare, social justice, acts of loving kindness, humanitarianism are not neutral terms that can be handled with frosty detachment. T. S. Eliot already observed that "social justice" is a much abused phrase; its rational content is often replaced by an emotional charge. This could be especially applicable in our case, for the Jewish tradition of social welfare contains much vitality, virtuosity, and relevance and can easily beget impassioned rhetoric. If, as Whitehead aphorized, all of Western thought is a footnote to Plato, one might suggest that western *humanitas* is a footnote to the Bible, and then proceed indolently to luxuriate in this flattering fact.

In this article I wish to answer three questions which presumably provide a matrix for comprehensive analysis of the issue under consideration. I have tried only to fulfill the function of a cartographer and plot the conceptual-historical terrain. The general scheme, worked out in terms of halakic categories, and in light of historic experiences, needs thoughtful elaboration and patient application to the many details of the problem. These three questions may be formulated as follows:

(1) What is the metaphysical foundation or ideological root of charity? Into what conceptual-axiological framework does the practice of philanthropy fit? (And let me hasten to add that this is not a purely speculative matter, for, as is always the case, the halakah consistently translates metaphysical postulates into practical conclusions.)

(2) Is charity, as conceived and nurtured in halakic thought, an integrated-unified act on the part of the individual or is it polaric and tense? Is it a simple, one-dimensional deed or a complex dialectical performance? In other words, just how much — in quantity and quality — does philanthropy demand from the individual?

(3) Is charity a particularistic performance of the Jew — like Sabbath observance — or is it a universal expression of the basic dignity of man and the concomitant sense of reciprocal helpfulness? On the practical level, this question revolves around the historic position of Judaism vis-a-vis non-Jewish philanthropic enterprises. It eventually asks how the activities of a welfare state fit into this framework.

Let us eliminate the third question for the time being — because of limitations of space — and concentrate on the remaining two.

The Jewish theory of philanthropy (*tzedakah; hesed*) or humanity, i.e. helping those who need help, has often been discussed — sometimes analyzed. Its centrality in Jewish life (and its concomitant importance in Jewish literature), starting in the Biblical period and continuing through Talmudic times into the modern era, is copiously documented. Many rabbinic statements which stress, with much verve and persuasiveness, the axial role of *hesed* are frequently quoted. You all know the dictum that "charity is equivalent to all the other religious precepts combined" (*Baba Batra,* 9a), or that "He who is merciful to others, mercy is shown to him by Heaven, while he who is not merciful to others, mercy is not shown to him by Heaven" (*Shabbat,* 151b). I have no intention of reviewing all this. My aim is simply to describe the metaphysical foundation of charity and underscore a few basic concepts, whose implications for Jewish social justice and welfare are as profound as they are pervasive, by interpreting one striking Talmudic passage. This is presented as a dialogue between the second-century sage R. Akiba and the Roman General Tineius Rufus who was appointed governor of the Judean province. This historical fragment embodies the quintessence of a Judaic social ethic : (a) the special role of man (in the world) resulting from his practice of philanthropy, and (b) the relation of men to each other.

It has been taught : R. Meir used to say : The critic [of Judaism] may bring against you the argument, "If your God loves the poor, why does he not support them?" If so, answer him, "So that through them we may be saved from the punishment of Gehinnom." This question was actually put by Tineius Rufus to R. Akiba : "If your God loves the poor, why does He not support them?"

He replied, "So that we may be saved through them from the punishment of Gehinnom."

"On the contrary," said the other, "it is this which condemns you to Gehinnom. I will illustrate by a parable. Suppose an earthly king was angry with his servant and put him in prison and ordered that he should be given no food or drink, and a man went and gave him food and drink. If the king heard, would he not be angry with him? And you are called servants, as it is written, *For unto me the children of Israel are servants."*

R. Akiba answered him : "I will illustrate by another parable. Suppose an earthly king was angry with his son, and put him in prison and ordered that no food or drink should be given to him, and someone went and gave him food and drink. If the king heard of it, would he not send him a present? And we are called sons, as it is written, *Sons are ye to the Lord your God.*"

He said to him : "You are called both sons and servants. When you carry out the desires of the Omnipresent, you are called 'servants.' At the present time you are not carrying out the desires of the Omnipresent."

R. Akiba replied : "The Scripture says, *Is it not to deal thy bread to the hungry and bring the poor that are cast out to thy house.* When dost thou bring *the poor who are cast out to thy house*? Now; and it says [at the same time], Is it not to deal thy bread to the hungry?"

(1)   The first premise to emerge from this dialogue is that *hesed* is that distinctive function which legitimatizes our worldly existence and adds a new dimension of purposiveness to life. It constitutes a special challenge and unique prerogative for man by establishing him as a very powerful agent and delicate instrument in the conduct of human affairs. God has abdicated part of a function of His in order to enable man to continue and extend creation. It is our practice of kindness which makes us continuators of God's creative plan, elevates our life from brutishness to sensitivity, and extricates us from chaotic, vacuous biological existence. Indeed, man was created only on the assumption that he would passionately pursue *hesed* and this, in turn, saves him from damnation and perdition.

This axial role of *hesed* is underscored in many other ways, among which the following is probably the most notable. While all religious-ethical actions are based on the principle of "imitation of God" (*imitatio dei* or *mimesis theou*), of walking in His ways and assimilating His characteristics, this is especially true of *hesed* in its broadest sense. *Hesed* is the most emphatic of God's attributes (rav *hesed*); the world came into existence because of it; the majority of God's actions toward man are characterized by it. The Torah begins and ends with loving kindness as a divine act. The practice of *hesed* thereby becomes man's "most God-like act."

However, this is not the complete picture. Aiding the needy in all forms is not only a fulfillment of *imitatio dei* but it is comparable to aiding God Himself. The same R. Akiba, whose dialogue with Rufus we are trying to interpret, dramatically deepens the social ethos of Judaism by equating charity to the poor with a loan to God! We are accustomed, on the basis of halakic terminology and conceptualization, to thinking of God as the ultimate "recipient" or "beneficiary" of all things "consecrated" for the Temple or other religious causes, all priestly gifts (tithe, heave-offering, etc.). God is the juridical personality that is the "owner" and all legal procedures are based on this fact. Now, in R. Akiba's homily, God appears also as the ultimate "beneficiary" of gifts to the poor. This involvement of God is certainly the noblest endorsement of that loving kindness practised between men.

(2)   Now, let us return to the second feature of the dialogue. At issue between the two discussants is the point of departure for determining human relationships. For R. Akiba we are all brothers, because we are all children and therefore completely equal before God. The brotherhood of man and fatherhood of God are inseparable. Any system which denies the common origin of man in God eviscerates the idea of brotherhood. Any system which affirms it must logically and inevitably sustain its corollary. The coordinates of the human system, in this view, are both horizontal and vertical, and together create a relationship which results in mutual responsibility and overlapping concern for each other. Even in a period of disgrace, disenchantment, or repudiation (such as exile or impoverishment), this relationship is not nullified and its demands not relaxed. Our identity as children and brothers is

never obscured. It is notable that the author of this statement, the great martyr who witnessed and experienced persecution and bestiality, was the one who articulated: "Beloved is man who was created in the image of God." His ethical objectivity was unaffected by oppression; his view of man and his heirarchy of values was firm.

For Rufus, on the other hand, only one aspect of the *vertical* relationship between man and God is determinative: that of submission and slavery. And had not Aristotle already proclaimed that "slaves are like animals?" And had not Plato defined the slave as a "species of tame animals?" If, then, the world is a large household inhabited by a mass of unrelated individuals—mere biological atoms—there can be no community of interests and responsibilities, no compassion and cooperation.

(3) Implicit in R. Akiba's exchange with the Roman governor of Palestine is also a realistic-pragmatic view of the human situation, a view which is sensitively attuned to suffering and privation and earnestly questing for improvement and fulfillment. The discussion here is not oriented to metaphysics; it is geared to ethics, to concrete social problems—something which is characteristic of Talmudic discussion generally. It implies that one cannot conveniently fall back upon religious assumptions in order to justify passivity and resignation when confronted with ethical and social indignities. We must not look upon trouble impassively, whether the motivation be determinism (this is God's decree) or condescension (some people are irretrievably singled out for subjection) or contemptuousness (physical-carnal matters are insignificant). Poverty and inequality are pervasive—and will perhaps endure forever—but they must be incessantly condemned and combatted. Judaism insists that man is obligated to mitigate injustice and alleviate suffering. There is, if you like, something

antithetical in this situation. Poverty or sickness may be viewed
as divine punishment or a form of retribution just as both
wealth and health may be construed as signs of divine favor or
reward. Indeed, given a theocentric, teleological view of life,
every episode or situation — exile, death — is divinely purposive.
Man, however, must not sit in judgment from such a theistic
perspective; it is not for him to approach poverty or sickness
as predetermined criminal or punitive situations. A provi-
dential view of history is no excuse for quietism or pretext
for withdrawal.

(4) Similarly, it seems to follow that one cannot dismiss
a destitute person with a counterfeit expression of faith:
"Rely on God, your father and king. He will help you." The
cherished virtue of *bitahon,* trust, is something with which to
comfort yourself in a time of depression, but it is not a pain-
killing drug to be callously prescribed for others. If Reuben
is starving, Simeon must provide food, not sanctimony. It is
true that Reuben must live with hope and courage, but Simeon
must act with dispatch and compassion. God's inscrutable
benevolence is not a substitute for man's tangible benevolence.
As Bahya ibn Pakuda observes, *bitahon* has a multiplicity of
implications: to the impoverished person it conveys the need
of tranquility, patience, and contentment with one's portion;
while to the man of means it suggests the obligation of sustained and gracious liberality.

Our cursory analysis of these four concepts implicit in
R. Akiba's dialogue enables us, in conclusion, to pinpoint the
unique feature of *hesed,* in contradistinction to other philanthropic systems. It would be gratuitous — and chauvinistic — to
give Judaism an exclusive monopoly over the practice of
charity; the rabbis, as a matter of fact, never denied that other
nations were charitable. Judaism's contribution is a new *motive*
for philanthropy: the religious-humane motive, which means

acting for the sake of humanity because of religious conviction and obligation. Humanity is an expression of piety ("Everyman who is endowed with loving kindness is without doubt a God-fearing man," *Sukkah,* 49b); the two are absolutely inseparable. Commitment to God is inconceivable in Judaism without compassion for man. "Whoever turns away his eyes from [one who appeals for] charity is considered as if he were serving idols" (*Baba Batka,* 10a). Philo describes philanthropy as "the virtue closest akin to piety, its sister, and its twin," for "the nature which is pious is also humane, and the same person will exhibit both qualities of holiness to God and justice to man." One cannot claim to be God-intoxicated without having an unquenchable thirst for social justice. Indeed, theological postulates sundered from their practical consequences are powerless, and — perhaps — purposeless. They are mutually supplementary and independently fragmentary.

This motive should be the propelling force of federation activities and should determine its welfare program.

Halakah is a tense, vibrant, dialectical system, identifiable by its beautiful blend of romanticism and classicism. This is both cause and consequence of the Halakah's insistence upon normativeness in action and inwardness in feeling and thought. The historic achievement of Halakah was to move beyond theoretical principles of faith to a minutely regulated code of religio-ethical behavior — to give concrete and continuous expression to theological ideals, ethical norms, and historical concepts. It is based upon the conviction that abstract belief, even an intensely personal or charismatic one, will be evanescent and that religious insight which is not firmly anchored down by practice is unreal. Its goal is spirituality together with conformity — "the saturation and transfusion of everyday life with the thought of God" (the felicitous phrase of a nineteenth-century Christian theologian, Bousset). This insistence upon the "coincidence of opposites" (call it law and prophecy if you like, or institution and charisma—everyday life and the thought of God) creates the "dialectical pull" or tension which is characteristic of so many root practices and fundamental beliefs of Judaism.

A favorite example of this creative tension is the institution of prayer, which attempts to balance inward experience with routinized performance, to avoid an anarchic liturgy, and at the same time not to produce a spiritless stereotype. In other words, the Halakah takes a thesis—spontaneity of prayer, manifest in a genuinely dialogic relationship between man and God—superimposes upon it an antithesis—standardization and uniformity of prayer—and strives to maintain a synthesis: a devotional routine.

I would like to suggest that the institution of *Tzedakah*, charity, provides an equally attractive illustration of this dialectical structure. The Halakah undertook to convert an initially amorphous, possibly even capricious, act into a rigidly defined and totally regulated performance. It made charitable contributions, usually voluntary in nature, obligatory—subject to compulsory assessment and collection. However, while objectifying and concretizing a subjective, fluid state of mind, it insisted relentlessly upon the proper attitude, feeling, and manner of action. It hoped to combine the thesis of free, spontaneous giving with the antithesis of soulless, obligatory contribution and produce a composite act which is subjective though quantified, inspired and regular, intimate yet formal. As is the case with prayer and other products of such dialectical synthesis, the tension is very great, for the breakdown of the synthesis is always an imminent and immanent possibility. The pattern of behavior may become atrophied and de-spiritualized or else the standardized practice may be overthrown. Here the tension is even reflected semantically in the term *Tzedakah* which is both righteousness and charity; an act based on one's moral conscience as well as an appropriate course of action spelled out in detail by the law.

Within the practical-Halakic framework of philanthropy, this polarity comes to the surface in two main areas. First of all, there is the constant interplay between the individual and the community with regard to the responsibility for and awareness of philanthropic needs. A study of the laws of charity yields paradoxical conclusions. On one hand, it seems that the central figure is the individual: to him are the commandments addressed. He is enjoined to engage unstintingly in charity work, and assiduously to help his fellow man. He is the hero of philanthropy, seeking exposure to needy people and responding effusively to their requests. On the other hand, it is surprising to find that the Halakah has assigned an indispensable, all-inclusive role to the community. The community acts not only as a supervisory enforcing agency but occupies the center of the stage as an entity possessed of initiative and charged with responsibility. One may persuasively argue that the Halakah makes of philanthropy a collective project: philanthropic endeavor, long-term aid (*kupah*) as well as immediate emergency relief (*tamhuy*), is thoroughly institutionalized. Responsibility for the care of the needy — sick, poor, aged, disturbed — is communal. The individual makes his contribution to the community chest and with this he apparently discharges his obligations. He acts mechanically, almost anonymously, by responding to the peremptory demand of the collectors "who go about among the people every Friday soliciting from each whatever is assessed upon him" (*Mishneh Torah, Hilkot Matenot Aniyim*). *Tzedakah* thus emerges as an individual obligation which is fulfilled corporately. And it should be noted that this is a premeditated arrangement. The community does not step in and assume responsibility ex post facto, after individuals have shirked their duty or failed to manage matters properly. The community initially appears as a modified welfare city-state, with its special functionaries who collect the compulsory levy and act as trustees for the poor and needy. This is the first expression of polarity between the individual and community.

Whoever continues to acquaint himself with *Hilkot Tzedakah* in the *Shulhan Aruk* or *Matenot Aniyim* in the *Mishneh Torah* comes across another basic antithesis inherent in the very concept of charity. On one hand, the Halakah is interested only in the objective act, the amount given, meeting the challenge, and relieving the needs of the destitute. This is a complete, self-contained, and determinate act. On the other hand we are confronted by an exquisitely sensitive Halakah, very much concerned not only with *what* but *how* the act of charity is implemented. Not only is the outward act important but the experiential component is significant. One need not rely upon the preacher's eloquence or the moralist's fervor to underscore the importance of motivation and attitude in the Halakic act of charity.

This correlation of the objective and subjective components within the individual act is the second area of tension and polarity.

Let us take up these two points briefly and concretize them somewhat. We may illustrate the polarity of the community-individual partnership by introducing a few specific laws.

For example, the Mishnah states that twelve months' residence is required before a man is counted as one of the townsmen and is obliged to support communal projects. The Talmud, however, goes on to cite another passage which differentiates between various levies. "A man must reside in a town thirty days to become liable for contributing to the soup kitchen, three months for the charity box, . . . and twelve months for contributing to the repair of the town walls." The reason for the distinction between charity and communal enterprises is clear. Only after a man has become a full-fledged resident and has submitted to communal jurisdiction does he become liable to abide by communal ordinances (*takkanot bene ha-ir*) and share communal expenses. Charity, though, is an individual obligation and one need not come under communal jurisdicition to be liable. The community, however, serves as the executive branch which organizes and implements and distributes.

The sense of communal involvement is projected even more in the following laws. "If the inhabitants of a city impose a charitable levy upon a visiting merchant, the contribution belongs to the poor of the city visited. If, however, the levy be imposed upon a visiting group of people, the contributing is done in the city visited, but the sum collected is conveyed, by the returning visitors, to the city of their origin that the poor of the latter city may be aided with that money." Again, the reason for the differentiation between a wayfaring individual and an itinerant company is apparent. The individual relates to his immediate communal framework and his charitable contribution is absorbed and disbursed there. A group of people, however, are considered to have affiliations with both communities. They contribute immediately to demonstrate their solidarity with the new group and remove suspicion that they are tax dodgers, but return the money for distribution to their original community. What is significant is the involvement with the community on all levels—the strong sense of community action.

So far the enterprising community is in the center and the timid individual is on the periphery. It would almost appear as if a man's obligation is terminated when he weighs the gold pieces or signs a check—and then, losing his identity, just fades away into the shadows of the community. Now let us see how the relationship shifts gear and hear the Halakah insist that there are aspects of the commandment concerning charity which transcend the basic levy exacted by the community. The institution of *kupah* relieves only one's minimal quantified duties but other individual contingent obligations are not superseded.

For example, the obligation of charity is based on both positive and negative commandments: "open thy hand unto him" — "thou shalt not harden thy heart nor shut thy hand" (cf. Leviticus, 25 : 35; Deuteronomy, 15 : 7–8). The nature of the relationship between such mutually reinforcing formulations — a *mizvat aseh* and a *mizvat lo ta aseh* — presents an Halakic problem. Some interpretations submit that the two are completely commensurate and the negative one has no intrinsic significance; it relates only to the omission of the positive — the failure to contribute. According to many Talmudic authorities, however, the negative commandment not to harden one's heart relates exclusively to one's mental-emotional attitude when confronted with distress. It is addressed only to the individual and stipulates that the individual should not be insensitive and non-responsive to the plea of an indigent person — "a poor person in search of help." The positive commandment is in no way contingent upon the plea or request of the poor, while the negative commandment relates not only to the omission of the positive but is also an act of commission: of callously refusing the poor, of consciously hardening one's heart and thwarting one's inclination to kindness.

What is more, if one has already given charity, even oversubscribed his quota, there is an additional law which states: "It is forbidden to turn away a suppliant poor person empty handed, though one grant no more than a single berry." This is based upon Psalm 74 : 21 "Let not the oppressed turn back in confusion."

The emphasis upon the individual responsibility is thus unequivocal. However, if you are not convinced, we might go further and submit that according to the social ethos of Judaism, the individual can never really isolate himself from the needy — *especially* in times of euphoria, pleasure, and indulgence. The very nature of rejoicing and festivity includes sharing with others. This axiom of kindness was formulated by Maimonides as follows. "While one eats and drinks by himself, it is his duty to feed the stranger, the orphan, the widow, and other poor and unfortunate people, for he who locks the doors to his courtyard and eats and drinks with his wife and family, without giving anything to eat and drink to the poor and the bitter in soul — his meal is not a rejoicing in a divine commandment, but a rejoicing in his own stomach . . . Rejoicing of this kind is a disgrace to those who indulge in it."

It is noteworthy that in many cities — one of the earliest records is from Hamburg — a communal ordinance required every townsman to have two guests for the Sabbath. Personal contact with and exposure to the needy was of the essence. "There was a certain pious man with whom Elijah used to converse until he made a porter's lodge (gatehouse) after which he did not converse with him any more" (because the poor men were shut out from the courtyard). Sharing the companionship of the poor and making them socially equal is a highly sensitive performance which merits special blessing. "He who lets poor people and orphans partake of food and drink at his table shall call upon the Lord and find, to his delight, that the Lord will answer." (Isaiah 58 :9.)

So although the balance may be delicate and tense, corporate responsibility does not eclipse individual awareness and should not dull individual sensitiveness. This would remain true even if communal funds were somehow (because of welfare contributions, for example) to be inexhaustible; individual obligations never cease.

Let us return to the second expression of polarity—the objective act vis-a-vis the inner experience and accompanying attitude. As a general principle we may study the assertion that "the reward of charity depends entirely upon the extent of the kindness in it" (*Sukkah,* 49b). The cold, formal, objective act does not suffice; it must be fused with warmth and loving kindness. From an objective point of view, the giving of charity is not subject to qualifications; if you give, that's that and the amount is the only thing that counts. From a subjective point of view, the same act may well be shoddy and meretricious. There can be such a thing as "defective charity." The difference is, if you like, whether there is a heart of flesh or a heart of stone behind it. Allow me to suggest perhaps that the difference expresses itself in the two expressions we have for this act : "giving charity" and "doing charity." "Doing" relates to the method and quality of "giving." "Giving" is concrete and limited; you give ten dollars or one hundred dollars. *Doing* is how you go about it.

A late source gives this apt illustration : "The giving is *Tzedakah.* [The doing is] the *trouble* to bring it to the poor man's house, or the *thought*fulness on the part of the giver that it should be most useful . . . in short, being *preoccupied* with the good of the poor recipient." The key terms here are *tirhah* and *tirdah,* which denote constant concern and abiding interest —continuous commitment rather than fleeting attention. The same idea of mental and emotional preoccupation is underscored by the recurrent idiom "osek be-Torah uvigmilut hasadim." *Osek* suggests a resilient, incompressible quality of attention and dedication; it negates the idea of a perfunctory, quantified act.

There are a number of specific *subjective* features which

may be collated under this general principle — that "the reward of charity depends entirely upon the extent of the kindness in it." Many of these features are embodied in Maimonides' original well-known classification of the "eight degrees of benevolence, one above the other." Instead of reproducing this classification here, it might be more useful to abstract from it and related source material a few characteristics and tendencies which identify the experiential component of charity.

(1)   Most important is to approach the needy prudently and tactfully and graciously: "happy is he that considereth the poor" (Psalm 41:2). The ultimate aim of this approach is to get the poor one to take a loan or else think that he is taking a loan; to accept him into business partnership or help him find employment. This completely eliminates or deftly camouflages humiliation and degradation. It rehabilitates rather than aids and avoids the most objectionable influences of pauperism. In other words, it is not only ethically correct but is also economically sound. Is not this the ideal of all philanthropic federations?

(2)   If the humiliation attendant on receiving charity cannot be eliminated, it should be reduced as much as possible. This expresses itself above all in the secrecy and privacy of giving. "He who gives alms in secret is greater than Moses."

(3)   Another basic principle is the insistence upon individual consideration of the needy rather than indiscriminate handling of them as so many "faces in the crowd." The indigent remains a dignified individual, with his own needs and drives, his own sensibilities and rights, strengths and weaknesses. The essence of the religious commandment is "to assist a poor person according to his needs" — in other words, selectively not uniformly. Regimentation or massive institutionalization are not

in keeping with this spirit. You might find here an inferential endorsement of the case-method of social work, being careful not to de-personalize the individual client or blur his identity by mechanically bracketing him. If you like, we have here the social-philanthropic repercussions of the metaphysical idea of the dignity, worth, and uniqueness of each individual.

(4) Also imperative is prompt courteous attention, with little or no red tape, bureaucratic inefficiency, or personal procrastination. Delay in responding to a request may blemish the entire act or even tragically obviate its need. You know the "confession" of the sorely afflicted Nahum ish Gamzu, who was "blind in both his eyes, his two hands and legs were amputated, and his whole body was covered with boils." He had wished this state upon himself after "a poor man stopped me on the road and said, Master give me something to eat. I replied : Wait until I have unloaded something from the ass. I had hardly managed to unload something when the man died" (*Ta amit* 21a).

(5) The benevolent act should be gracious from beginning to end and should not display half-heartedness or impatience. It is in this light that we understand one of the commandments subsumed under the precept "Love thy neighbor as thyself," namely the obligation to "escort strangers and departing guests." "Hospitality to wayfarers is greater than receiving the Divine Presence . . . but escorting guests is even greater than according them hospitality. . . . Whoever does not accompany guests is as though he would shed blood" (*Hilkot Abel*, XIV, 2). It would appear that hospitality without escorting is like throwing a bone to a dog — a begrudging concession of kindness, an intrinsically benevolent act which is vitiated by its rudeness.

(6)   Most striking because it is most intangible and "supra-legal" is the stipulation that actual giving be accompanied by sympathy, sharing the recipient's troubles, talking with him, relieving him psychologically. It calls for a genuine sense of commiseration. "He who gives a small coin to a poor man obtains six blessings, and he who addresses to him words of comfort obtains eleven blessings." Maimonides sharpens this sentiment even more : "Though one were to give a thousand pieces of gold, one forfeits, yea, one destroys the merit of one's giving if one gives grudgingly and with countenance cast down." On the contrary, "one should give cheerfully and eagerly. One should grieve with the poor person over his misfortune (Job 30 : 25) and should address to him words of solace and of comfort" (Job 29 : 13).

The receiver must feel that there is a living human voice behind the grant, not a hollow, impersonal one. The donor should never lose sight of the fact that *Tzedakah* is as much a "duty of the heart" as it is a "duty of the limb."

Without these subjective elements, the objective act is deficient and sometimes even worthless.

Even though we have expanded its scope and insisted upon the place of subjectivity in it, we have been talking almost exclusively about *Tzedakah*. However, we should not fail to note that there is within the scope of *hesed* an entire area of acts of kindness where the personal subjective attitude is not only relevant but is of exclusive significance. This may be designated as "mental hygiene" (as distinct from physical aid and rehabilitation). Of the several categories of kindness referred to in the Talmud, two belong to this area : visiting the sick, comforting the bereaved. These acts could also conceivably be regulated — e.g., stipulating by communal ordinance that the sick should be visited right after the Sabbath morning service — but clearly the physical act of entering the sick room, unlike the physical act of signing a check, is worthless. For these are "the deeds of loving kindness performed in person and for which no fixed measure is prescribed." The subjective moment is paramount.

Old-age care and consideration is another area in the realm of kindness and social welfare where the attitude outweighs or at least conditions the act. This is true with regard to parents as well as aged people generally. We are obliged "to rise up before the grey-haired and honor the face of the old man." There is nothing material in this. Financial assistance to poor old people is to be viewed from the general vantage point of charity. The specific obligation is the reverential attitude : to stand, to make respectful gestures. With regard to one's parents, the material assistance, when required, is probably also to be viewed from the vantage point of charity. Indeed, the Halakah states that honoring one's parents means providing them with food and drink, clothing and covering, but the expense is to be borne by the parents. What counts, on the part of the son, is the zeal and quality of service. In other words, the fulfillment of "honoring thy father and mother" and "ye shall fear, every man, his mother and father" is not contingent upon finance. Indeed, since it was emphatically maintained that the honoring of parents was on a level with the honoring of God, this could not be, in essence, a materially conditioned act. In socially ideal situations, where the parents have independent resources, the duty of honor and reverence is unimpaired and their scope unrestricted. The religious-social obligations toward an old person are the same regardless whether he is independently wealthy, sustained by social security and old-age assistance, or indigent.

In this sense, welfare activities, which tend to mitigate financial difficulties, cannot be looked upon as corrosive of traditional values and obligations because they do not impinge upon the core of philanthropic actions : the motif of personal service and attitude. Welfare activities are no more "dangerous" in theory than the activities of high-powered, mechanized philanthropy: both challenge the subjective element, tend to neutralize or obliterate it. The response to this challenge will have to reaffirm that if Halakah, generally, was intended to be a continuing education in holiness and spiritual dedication, *Tzedakah* in particular was intended to be an education in kindness and all-consuming *humanitas*.

5

Judaism and Mental Health

A distinguished panel of rabbis, psychiatrists, and lay leaders met together in a profoundly significant pioneer program in the sharing of psychiatric experiences, insight, professional skills, and knowledge in matters of mutual concern. The discussion of the varied aspects of the relationships between mental health and Judaism is scintillating and seminal as it brings both the wisdom of the sages of the Beth Hamedrash and of psychiatry together for a sharp and illuminating humanistic, religious, legal, and medical focus on problems of human behavior, neuroses, and the disintegration and reintegration of the personality. The result is an outstandingly revealing, provocative colloquy and sharing of expert views, insights and knowledge.

The voluntary nature of Jewish life under the conditions of democracy has been inimical to the transplantation of the Kehillah of the European dispersion. In response to the new conditions of life and its accompanying psychic strains, the

American Jewish community has responded with all the skills of social welfare and mental health. However, the mutual dialogue which follows places the community approach to mental health in dealing with Jews on a completely new and creative plane in which Judaism itself becomes a significantly valuable context which the practising, understanding psychiatrist can apply for beneficial prognostic and therapeutic purposes.

MENTAL HEALTH AND JUDAISM : A SYMPOSIUM

For the first time in the history of this, the largest Jewish community in the United States, there has been a planned effort to formally bring together for a symposium, conducted under communal sponsorship, leaders of the rabbinate and the laity with practicing experts in mental health.

The result of this dialogue was a pioneer conference on Mental Health and Judaism, marked by a sharing of experiences, insights, and their professional skills and knowledge by distinguished New York psychiatrists and psychoanalysts in mental health problems of mutual concern to religious and lay representatives.

The valuable perceptions precipitated by this dialogue have vital meaning for Jewish social welfare agencies, and particularly those with mental health caseloads. For psychiatrically oriented social workers, especially in Jewish family counseling agencies, who are again and again confronted with the various aspects of the relationship between mental health and Judaism, such shared dialogues are illuminatingly helpful.

The symposium participants were : Rabbis Ben Zion Bokser, Forest Hills, N.Y.; Robert Gordis, Temple Beth El of Rockaway Park, N.Y., and Professor of Bible at Jewish Theological Seminary; Rabbi David I. Golovensky, Beth El Synagogue, New Rochelle, N.Y.; Rabbi Edward Sandrow, Temple Beth

El, Cedarhurst, L.I.; Rabbi David Seligson, Central Synagogue, Manhattan; Judge Matthew M. Levy, Justice of the Supreme Court, State of New York, Chairman of the Committee on Religious Affairs, Federations of Jewish Philanthropies; Drs. Abram Franzblau, Mt. Sinai Hospital; Morris Hinenberg, Federation of Jewish Philanthropies; Abram Kanof, Professor of Pediatrics, State of New York Medical School; Raymond Nadell, Downstate Medical Center; Montagu Ullman, Maimonides Hospital. Rabbi Henry Kagan, Sinai Temple, Mt. Vernon, N.Y., served as Moderator.

The discussion follows:

DR. ROBERT GORDIS : We are engaged in a pioneering venture, and therefore I suppose that there will inevitably be a good deal of lost motion involved until we sort of find our bearings and begin to focus on the matter at hand. There are several fundamental caveats that have to be borne in mind before we discuss the Jewish concept of guilt. First, the Jewish tradition itself is not monolithic, and therefore it is not easy to structure the Jewish concept of guilt. In fact, among Jewish scholars and thinkers there are two points of view as to the nature of the Jewish tradition itself. There are some very distinguished thinkers who believe that Judaism is a stream of many currents and that it is unfair to speak of any as more normative than others. My own view is that there is a mainstream; even though there are also subordinate streams, it is still possible in some sense to define the fundamental trend, while allowing always for variations on the fringes. If this were not so it would be more difficult to deal with the subject of the Jewish concept of guilt.

Second, Judaism suffers from another innate characteristic — it rarely deals with abstract categories; therefore, to define the attitude of Judaism toward guilt, or any other theme for that matter, is essentially a task of reconstruction. It must be derived from concrete incidents and specific legal enactments to be found in the practical literature of the Bible and the Talmud and the post-Talmudic period. Sometimes there is of course the natural risk that we may be not reading out of the tradition but reading into the tradition — engaging in what the scholars call not merely exegesis but eisagesis; and that a risk which is very genuine.

Further, living as we do in a civilization where Christianity is dominant, and in view of the term "Judaeo-Christian tradition," many of us are prone to make the mistake of assuming that Judaism and Christianity operate with the same fundamental values everywhere. Now, I do not share the point of view that there is no such thing as a Judaeo-Christian tradition, but it is important to realize that while there is a common heritage which the two great religions of the Western world share, they are by no means identical. Actually, in certain fundamental areas, of which guilt is one, there is a radical divergence between Judaism and Christianity. That is why you simply cannot extract categories of thought from Christianity and assume that they are, without too much consideration, identical in Judaism.

This is particularly true on such subjects as human nature in general and marriage and guilt in particular.

For a good number of years I have been an interested lay-amateur student of psychology. I have attempted to utilize whatever understanding I have of it in my own fields, which are linguistics, Biblical interpretation, and contemporary religion. However, I do not claim any technical competence in this field, so that every statement I make is prefaced by the words "I believe," subject to the reader's correction and elucidation.

Judaism and Psychiatry are in some respects parallel in their understanding of guilt and in some respects they diverge. Both these disciplines believe that guilt is subject to therapy; it is not something which is beyond reconstruction and rehabilitation. But there is a radical difference in temper and content. Perhaps it could be perceived by saying that Judaism is not concerned basically with "guilt feelings" but with guilt. It is aware of the fact that there are guilt feelings, and it is interested in them because it is concerned with people; but it is especially concerned with guilt itself, not with guilt feelings. For the psychiatrist, guilt feelings would seem to be an objective reality. With regard to guilt, he may have his own opinions whether there is such a thing as guilt or not. To the extent that the discipline is concerned, guilt feelings have objective reality — that is as far as the psychiatrist is ready to go. But for Judaism, guilt itself is a basic reality which must be removed.

This is a far-reaching distinction which deserves further exploration. Judaism generally does not regard "guilt" but "sin" as the most fundamental concept. The Hebrew word for "guilt," *asham,* is much less frequent in our sources than the word *chet* which means "sin." So that Judaism, by using the word "sin," makes an assumption that there are moral standards of objective character, and the word "sin" enshrines this conception of the validity of these moral standards. The psychiatrist may or may not believe in such standards, but in his professional capacity he is essentially amoral or, to put it bluntly, he is "neutral" on the subject of his moral standards. He may set the concept of adjustment as his goal, or whatever other term may seem to him to be closest to the truth, but he is not as such an advocate of, or a believer in, moral standards. Judaism, however, very definitely is not neutral and distinctly believes that such moral standards exist, so that while Judaism is deeply sympathetic to human weaknesses, it regards the existence of standards as fundamental, and guilt or sin represents a falling away from these standards.

To cite some classic terms: the Hebrew word *Het,* or "sin," etymologically means "missing the mark." It is actually borrowed from archery in the oldest sources we have, and it suggests the idea that there is a mark that the marksman should have achieved, and that he just happened to miss it. So missing the mark is basic to the concept of guilt. Another word *avon* comes from the root which means "to pervert or twist" or in general "to distort." It again suggests the idea that there was something straight that the individual has perverted and distorted for reasons which of course have to be explored.

A third Hebrew term is *Pesha,* which means rebellion in its etymological sense, and it represents the theme of rebellion against legitimate authority. In this case the authority is the source of the moral law which is God. This is why the tradition regards the existence of these standards as possessing objective reality emanating from a divine source and man is regarded as responsible for adhering to and obeying these standards. When he doesn't, he has either missed the mark or he has perverted his essential nature, or he has rebelled against Him to whom obedience is due.

This approach is, for example, borne out in the book many peoples regard as the most skeptical of the Hebrew scriptures, the Book of Ecclesiastes, which contains this passage : "This I sought, but I found not; one man in a thousand I found [meaning one decent human being in a thousand], but one woman in a thousand I did not find (Ecclesiastes, 8 : 28). That is a very cynical statement, but notice the next verse (8 : 29): "Note this which I have seen, God has made man straight, but men have found many devices." In other words, even in this the most skeptical book within the tradition, the conception is that Man essentially, primordially is straight, not perfect. But for reasons which may or may not be susceptible to analysis, Man has perverted this essential quality of Mankind.

This leads to another observation that Judaism, unlike classical Christianity, is not preoccupied or rather "obsessed" with the concept of "innocence," but rather with the concept of "righteousness." Many have seen Arthur Miller's play *After the Fall*. This is treated by psychiatrists in a very interesting paper in a recent issue of *The Reconstructionist,* the issue of May 1, 1964. Dr. Nathaniel Lehrman, who makes an analysis of this play *After the Fall*, thinks that in this title of his play Arthur Miller means, by the word "Fall," "withdrawal from personal responsibility and the abandonment of courage in the moral law." Being somewhat more theologically oriented, that is not my view of what Miller means by this title. I saw the play and I read it, and my understanding is that Miller is using the term "After the Fall" in its classical Christian theological sense. Those of you who read or saw the play will remember how obsessed the hero is with "innocence": he is constantly engaged in looking for innocence — the innocence of course which was the estate of man before the act of disobedience by Adam in the Garden of Eden.

Now, if Miller were ideologically a Jew, he would of course not have attached such importance to innocence. He would have been concerned essentially with the concept of righteousness. For the Jewish tradition which lays great stress upon righteousness — *Tzedakah* — of which we are particularly conscious in this building of Federation. The word *Tzedakah,* which means "righteousness," is a basic Hebrew term, whereas for the term of "innocence," we actually have no abstract noun. We have *Naki,* an "innocent person." We do not even have an abstract term for it in Hebrew which indicates something of the degree to which Judaism does not concern itself with "innocence" *per se,* but with righteousness. This is the theme repeated again and again in Scriptures: "There is no man who is perfectly righteous and who doesn't commit sin." Innocence, we might almost be in a position to say, is not granted to Man, but righteousness, Judaism regards as being accessible to Mankind.

You will recall that St. Paul argued very strongly that this was a weakness in Judaism because it made a fetish of righteousness. But rightly or wrongly the Jewish tradition regards this as important.

This distinction between innocence and righteousness leads to a series of other distinctions in the Jewish tradition. Judaism does not equate feelings with actions. It does not say that a feeling is just as important as an act, and this is by no means a purely theoretical significance. Dr. Lehrman quotes a passage from Freud: "This equating of thoughts and deeds comes from Freud, who wrote: 'It is not really a decisive matter whether one has killed one's father or is saved from the deed. One must feel equally guilty in either case, for guilt is the expression of a conflict of ambivalence, the eternal struggle between Eros and the destructive or death instincts.'" What Dr. Lehrman attributes to Freud is here simply reproducing a New-Testament conception of which he may not have been aware. In Matthew 52:18 we are told that "He who looketh at a woman to lust after her hath committed adultery with her already in his heart."

If you operate with the concept of innocence then the thought of evil or the performance of evil does not differ very much, but if you operate with the concept of righteousness there is, of course, a tremendous difference between having the desire to kill one's father and actually committing the act; the Jewish tradition makes this clear distinction. It is true that Judaism opposes lustful thoughts. In the great passage in Job, chapter 31, in his famous confession of innocence, Job begins by saying: "I have made a covenant with mine eyes; and I have not looked lustfully on a maiden." But while the emphasis upon purity of thought is fundamental in Judaism, it does not therefore assume that thought and deed are of the same hierarchy of value or disvalue, as the case may be.

Of course once you make this assumption, that one must feel

equally guilty in either case, you are preparing yourself for the kind of position which Hannah Arendt adopted in connection with her now-famous study of the complicity of the Jewish victims in their own execution at the hands of the Nazis. Since all of us are to some degree guilty of wrong thoughts, and of acts of omission, permission and commission, one can arrive at the conclusion that the victim is as guilty as the criminal.

This type of moral nihilism is totally repugnant to Judaism. This concept, that there is no hierarchy of values Judaism rejects and, because it is a legalistic system, it may be one of the glories of the legalistic system, in that it does distinguish between a felony and a misdemeanor, between a major crime and a minor crime. Judaism does have standards in which it evaluates these things. It is fair to say that Judaism would regard errors of permission, omission, and commission all as sins, but it would not place them on the same level: it would not regard a sin of omission as being of the same seriousness as a sin of commission. It would not disregard a sin of permission, which is forbidden in our tradition. You remember the great passage in the nineteenth chapter of Leviticus: "Thou shalt not stand idly by the blood of thy neighbor." Yet Judaism does not regard that as being exactly the same as committing murder itself.

All these distinctions flow out to the recognition that the basic preoccupation of the Jewish tradition in the ethical realm is in the creation of righteous men and women. Not *innocent* men and women, not *perfect* men and women, but *righteous* men and women.

Judaism is aware of the obstacles to moral living that exist in human nature, and therefore it does not adopt a kind of facile optimism: the concept of the perfectibility of human nature. On the other hand it does not adopt the pessimistic conception of human nature — this notion of the inherent sin of man —

which goes back, of course, to the New Testament. Incidentally in Judaism the doctrine that the sin of Adam and Eve in the Garden of Eden, whether mythologically or literally conceived of, has no theological importance. In Christian theology, the doctrine of original sin is sometimes presented in simple form, as by fundamentalists; sometimes in a highly sophisticated form as by Reinold Neibuhr. Both these conceptions are actually an interpretation — a Christian interpretation read into the Biblical text.

In the Jewish tradition we conceive of human nature as possessing two basic impulses : the good impulse and the evil impulse. Judaism lays great stress upon the power of the evil impulse. It argues that the evil impulse if anything is even stronger in many respects than the good impulse. But at the same time it holds fast to its conviction, which is essentially an act of faith, that it is possible for man to overcome the evil impulse by means of the good impulse. Moreover, Judaism recognizes that the sources of evil impulse are sometimes economic and social and very often takes sexual forms. So much so that in Rabbinic Hebrew, *Yetzer hara,* the evil desire is a synonym for the sexual impulse, because the Hebrews knew how powerful it is and how very often it takes forms which are destructive of moral values.

At the same time, the Jewish tradition is well aware of the fact that the evil impulse *Yetzer,* including the sexual impulse, is itself an instrument of potential good. In several of the classical passages of the tradition this is emphasized — notably in the one which says that were it not for the evil impulse no man would build a house, or marry, or beget children, or engage in an occupation. In fact, we are commanded in the tradition actually to love God with both of these impulses, which means that these potentially dangerous impulses can become the instruments for the enhancement of life.

In sum, the Jewish tradition believes that therapy should

be available, not simply for the removal of "guilt feelings" but for the effort to remove the "guilt." The process of therapy in the Jewish religion is called *teshuvah* the word itself is important, it does not mean "penitence," which is related to the Latin word *poena*, "punishment" or "pain," but means "return." Again it emphasizes the idea that the sinner is one who has strayed from the path that he could have trodden, should have trodden, and can find again if he is prepared to do so.

In the process of penitence or *teshuvah* he requires first of all contrition—the confession of one's sins—and restitution of the evil done, so that the person can place himself at peace with God.

In a very important passage, the Talmud asks: What is the fate of the sinner? A variety of answers is offered by the various components of the Jewish tradition; one stated that the sinner must die facing the consequences of his evil, another declares that the sinner must bring a sacrifice and thus find atonement. The final answer is "Let him repent of his sins and he will ultimately reestablish his peace with God." It therefore seems clear that the teacher of Judaism has a contribution to make in cases which do not become pathological. Where the disharmony becomes pathological, it means that the teaching of religion is no longer able to take effect. That person needs the kind of professional guidance which the psychiatrist is uniquely equipped to offer. But before that acute level is reached, the teacher of religion—if he possesses two essential qualities of religion, "sympathy" and *sechel*—can do much to restore the moral health which is the prelude to mental health.

II

DR. ROBBINS : In general, Dr. Gordis' distinction in respect to the psychiatrist's being concerned primarily with the problem of feelings of guilt, as contrasted to "actual guilt," following the commission of a misdeed or a sin is basically correct. The psychiatrist is concerned primarily with people who suffer from feelings of guilt — which are expressions in our judgment of unconscious conflict — rather than feelings associated with acts, which violate the laws and rules of the society in which the individual lives. The psychoanalytic position is based upon a conflict between instinctual impulses on the one hand and the prohibitions of what we call the superego. The superego we know partially as the term "conscience." It is largely experientially derived, and consists to a large extent of the prohibitions, punishments, disapproval, feelings of threats of loss of love, as these are initially experienced by the child in relation to his parents. It isn't, however, totally derived from experience. As Rabbi Gordis indicated, there is the distinction between the concept of righteousness and the concept of innocence. Concerning man's drives, sexual impulse, and ultimately capacity for good as well as evil — which would fit the psychoanalytic concept of the instincts — there is some debate in psychoanalytic circles over the question of whether there is essentially one instinctual drive — mainly the erotic — and the concept of dual instincts — the erotic and the aggressive.

Psychoanalysis believes, as a result of clinical observations, that individuals are born with certain drives, tensions, or tendencies which on the one hand lead to close affectional relationships and on the other hand are destructive. In one sense these two are viewed as not entirely destructive. One has to kill to live — that is, one has to kill animals to eat — and you can say in the very primitive basic sense one cannot be completely altruistic and yet survive if one has equal respect for all forms of life.

However, one of the problems from the psychiatric and psychological point of view is that man is a herd animal that must learn to modify, curb, and adjust his instinctual impulses in accordance with the society he lives in. This is accomplished through a variety of growth experiences that inevitably lead to the formation of certain sets of rules, which are initially presented to the child both verbally and explicitly, and more subtly by parental attitudes. The parents, in a sense, are the initial interpretors to the child of what society permits or prohibits. It is hoped or anticipated that these instinctual drives will gradually come under the control of another part of the personality — that part we refer to as the ego. Hopefully it will be rational, and make appropriate adjustments to curb the instinctual drive at the behest of the physical reality, and at the behest of the culture or the society in which the individual lives. In many ways, the moral values of a particular culture and the religious ideas are presented to the child subtly, by attitude as well as by exposition and education. In fact, much more by the former than by the latter, the precepts or examples of parents become a very important part of the nucleus of what we refer to as the superego. Part of this is the conscience, part of this is intellectually understood, part of this is morally explicit and is that part of one's conscious sense of right and wrong which one knows or feels and is able to say to *oneself* (regardless of what one may say to others) how one feels about one's acts or behavior.

This adjustment is not achieved easily. First we must consider another basic aspect of the assumptions of psychoanalysis: that the primitive instinctual drives, even though they may come under the control of the ego and the superego, still exist — and will exist forever. These are biological "givens" and do not disappear; they are there today and will be tomorrow, and one has to build appropriate measures within his personality and life adjustment for the expression and gratification of these drives, which will ultimately be in consonance with one's own inner developed self and the society in which one lives. And when there is conflict or inability to effect a compromise that will provide appropriate gratification, appropriate sublimation, appropriate direct expression, and appropriate control then illness can ensue. If, for instance, the superego is in effect tyrannical; if it views every possible manifestation of the impulses as bad, as evil, regardless of how they are expressed, regardless of how they manifest themselves, and as something reprehensible, the individual may suffer from undue feelings of guilt.

Many individuals are bothered by an awareness, even though it may be unconscious, of certain drives and impulses which constantly evoke in them feelings of guilt, even though the probability of their ever committing an act based upon such impulse or feelings is remote or virtually impossible. We see in these people the great problem, which was referred to earlier, where there is an equation on the neurotic level between feeling or thinking of an evil act. If the act would be evil by the judgment of the individual, for most people it would make no difference whether society detects it and imposes its organized penalties upon it.

It is not certain in what context Dr. Lehrman quoted Freud. Freud said the equation of the feelings and the deed is a neurotic unconscious equation rather than a realistic healthy one. In fact, this is exactly one of the things which in psychotherapy one tries to help the patient realize that there is a vast difference between having an *impulse* to kill one's father and *killing* one's father. They are not at all alike. This is aside from what father may feel about it. It is an irrational primitive element of the unconscious that makes this equation and escapes the reality-testing capacity of the individual. This is one of the real efforts in psychotherapy. Secondly, it is also an aspect of psychotherapy to help the individual recognize that such impulses do exist, not only in himself but in other people. Hostile drives and sexual drives are not anything foreign to the human being. Here we have some harmony between today's concept of the inherent, I won't say original, sin. As was said, God made man straight but man has made many devices. I'm not sure that we would quite agree with that, but we *will* say that God has made man the way he is — with strong sexual urges, with strong hostile impulses — and in turn man and God together have imposed certain restrictions on the way in which these should be expressed. The sexual drives bring us together for constructive effort to be helpful and humanistic; they bring a man and a woman together to form the nucleus of a family. To this should be added the curious fact that when one works carefully with patients there is a tendency first to view the rigidity, the tyranny, the prohibitions of the superego as being entirely experientially determined. That is, these are a child's misinterpretation of the attitudes of his parents and they are incorporated into his own ideas before he is mature enough to make respectable and independent judgments and to modify them in terms of reality.

Unfortunately to a certain extent this is true. A parent may make a lot of prohibitions to a small child pending that child's having the capacity for discriminatory judgment: "you don't," "you must not," "you may not" — a series of categorical imperatives. Unfortunately what happens is that if the threat or fear engendered in the child by the prohibitions is great enough to repress the impulses and keep it unconscious they will not be available for later modification and a perfectly innocent impulse that is nevertheless prohibited, i.e., "don't suck your thumb," "you may not suck your thumb," is translated to, "you may never even smoke a cigarette."

The impulses thus escape the capacity of the maturing ego

to make subsequent effective discriminatory judgment, so that a lot of impulses become repressed and remain archaic and primitive and childish because they are separated from the learning that the child experiences throughout life as he grows. Therefore, on the one hand the severity of the superego and the fear that individuals have of punishment from the superego may be due to the primitive elaborate fantasies of the parent as a towering, big, and frightening person—the boogie man.

This isn't all that gives the power to the superego, for it has been postulated that very rarely is the severity of the superego a representative of the actual severity of the experiences of the child and the prohibitions brought to him by the world of his parents and other parental figures. Usually the superego is much more vicious, much more tyrannical, much more cruel, and much more demanding of its pound of flesh than anything the parents ever represented to the child. If one has the opportunity to get acquainted with mother and father and judge them realistically and accurately, usually one finds that the superego is an extension, a distortion, of them—even though there may often be a marked resemblance.

Now the question comes up : Where does this excessive attitude of the superego come from? And here's a very curious thing : the personality apparently borrows the hostility, which is primitive, and turns it against itself. Thus, much of the hostility that one feels toward one's own impulses is converted into a police force against oneself. The energy and the source come from the biological primitive instincts to begin with; added to, rationalized by, and augmented by the authority figures upon whom the child is initially dependent for love. Without the love, without the security to retain their love and interest he is helpless and lost, and therefore he must behave.

I think, then, that one of the problems that we see is how the child adds the religious teaching, adds the moral teaching, to the superego already there. Actually his religious moral preaching does not begin just when he is taught religion in the formal sense. By the time the child reaches this point in life the superego and its rigidity and its tyranny — if it is tyrannical — has pretty well developed. Religion can modify what is left to be modified, but religion by itself cannot relieve a sense of guilt, if the sense of guilt is derived from the superego. You can preach, you can educate, you can say, "look, you felt like it but you didn't do it," and the patient still suffers. If, on the other hand, it is a misinterpretation of society, a misinterpretation of things left later, then I think there is room for moral teaching and judgment. The clergyman's work is to a large extent more directed towards the ego, the psychiatrist's more towards the superego in terms of the element of conflict. All Freud said was, "that a feeling of guilt is just as real whether or not the person killed his father or thought he did," but he did *not* say these are equivalent and therefore the person is filled with guilt. If that was Lehrman's interpretation, he was wrong.

DR. GORDIS : There is a substantial measure of parallel ideas phrased by Dr. Robbins in a different idiom which can serve as a basis for operating together. The passage Dr. Lehrman quotes from Freud doesn't include the context, but the implication is that it is not the neurotic sufferer who equates it, but rather Freud himself. He says one must feel equally guilty in either case, for guilt is an expression of ambivalence. Dr. Robbins may be right in his interpretation of Freud and it is certainly very important to ascertain whether this is a neurotic confusion, and whether Freud himself thought so. But one thing is sure : there are certain religious traditions that do equate the two. Yes, then you might say that is an expression of a neurosis, but the passage in Matthew, for example, certainly does equate the two. There are other examples of it as well. So the argument itself is unaffected, whether it is

Freud who is guilty of that confusion, or the neurotic, or certain forms of religious tradition. When Dr. Robbins emphasizes that these instinctual forces remain, this conforms completely with the Jewish tradition. It regards this battle between the good impulse and evil impulse as lasting as long as life does. There is a very interesting passage in which the Talmud actually raises the question that if, when a man gets old, does he ever get beyond that stage; the argument is "No he never does."

Further, on the positive side, is the emphasis in the tradition which is repeated in Deuteronomy no less than three times: "Life and death I place before you this day." This passage emphasized again and again that the choice has to be made. Or, you might very well say the resolution of the conflict has to be made perpetually; it isn't limited; you don't conquer it; you cannot then afford to sit back feeling that the battle is over. Dr. Robbins also said that the superego has frequently developed long before formal religious training has taken place. This is a completely sound observation. We might wish to answer the question concerning the origin of the components of the superego. After all, religion is not limited to formal religious instruction, and in a certain sense it may be derived from religion in the primordial forms long before the child sits in the classroom, or is told by his father or mother "do this" or "don't do that," so that the role of religion may therefore for good and for ill be greater than that of the formal religious instruction. The last observation I would like to make is this: Dr. Robbins says that it isn't enough to say to the patient or the sufferer: "You didn't do it." He says the patient still feels bad. That is quite true; we have all had it in our own experience. I emphasize the role of Teshuba. According to the Jewish tradition, if a person comes and says "I committed this crime," or "I thought of this crime," one must not say: "You didn't do it," or "Other people have done it," and expect the person to be healed. Actually, one must take it very seriously.

During the dark days of the depression we had an old retired butcher in the congregation, whom I met shortly before the High Holy Days. He seemed very much depressed, and beginning a conversation with him I discovered that he had made no provision for worship on the High Holy Days. I said to him, "Well I'll be very happy to arrange for you to have a seat at services." He answered, "My wife, she bought one ticket. She won't have me there." It developed that there was a conflict in his home due to various forms of anxiety, breakup of support, and so on. Again, in the conversation with him, it turned out that he was suffering from the guilt feeling of thirty years before when he was a butcher on Third Avenue and had short-weighted the customers. I could have said to him quite honestly that every butcher does. It would have done him no good whatsoever, nor did I say to him "It was a minor matter, a matter of a few cents." I took it very seriously with him. I said, "That's a major offense. You've actually engaged in violating a Commandment by stealing. But in our religion there are forms of repentance to be made. You can't restore the money to all your customers of thirty years ago, but there are other things you can do." I proceeded to outline a regimen of observance for him, and I was actually able to restore him to sufficient skill to be able to operate, to get a job, and to work again, which he had been unable to do beforehand. Now, whether my methods were right or wrong, what the tradition would say is not to dismiss the sin as unimportant, but to say that although it is important there are avenues of regeneration that are open to you. That is what I meant when I spoke of therapy and I didn't have a chance, of course, to spell it out in greater detail.

DR. ROBBINS : First, let me comment on the butcher. The psychiatrist would raise the question: "Why did this bother him thirty years later?" The answer is that this would, in our judgment, probably represent rationalization for something else about which he was guilty and depressed, and it is very common for a depressed person in his fifties and sixties to say: "I masturbated when I was twelve years old, I'm no good," and ignore everything that's happened between.

You say, "Why now, why didn't he feel guilty at twelve or suffer depression then?" But I would agree, however, that where one encounters a person feeling real guilt over a real act, most psychiatrists cannot do anything about that except to help him find effective restitution in whatever form it is appropriate to take.

I have long learned that it is very rare or even effective to treat a person in lieu of a prison sentence if he feels guilty. It is much better to treat him after the prison sentence. I'm balancing this, but I hate like hell when courts say: "Well, go see the psychiatrist and then we'll decide if you're guilty," where it's not a question of insanity. Then he's got a choice of go to jail, or get psychiatric treatment, and I've actually had a patient who came into the hospital under those circumstances; he was getting nowhere in therapy, and he said finally: "Doctor, I think I'd better go back and serve my year and then I'll come back and see you."

I cannot accurately answer one other question — the source of the original components of superego. I don't know the source. Certainly it comes out of our culture in part. It comes out of a necessity, whatever culture you live in, to master primitive instincts; there is a great fear in all people of being overwhelmed by the primitive instincts, so the superego, in every culture, in every form, with every kind of institution you can think of — from prisons to religions — is the means of institutionalizing control over man's primitive instincts.

RABBI KAGAN : A president of a neighboring girls' college in my community asked one of his students to come to see me. She was a Jewish girl, who had finally achieved status by being admitted to the non-virgins club on the campus and her problem as she stated it was, "I feel guilty because I don't feel guilty." This is a kind of teenage beatnik refinement of the problem that the rabbi and the psychiatrist have been debating with us.

DR. NADELL : One of the things we have to consider when we talk about guilt and also the absence of guilt—something we all have to be concerned with, not merely as psychiatrists but also as human beings—is the fact that an absence of guilt would imply that the superego controls have not been built up and this can be a matter of failure of the family, or a failure of the community at large to train the individual. The consequent absence of guilt is something that is very often dumped onto the lap of psychiatrists. I am thinking of a recent situation where a judge suspended sentence on an individual who committed a sexual crime with the proviso that he go for psychiatric therapy for as long as his sentence would normally last. Here we were concerned with cultivating feelings of guilt in this individual so that his further actions would not repeat the crime for which he was originally sentenced.

Then, in the guilt itself we have a number of manifestations we have to consider. We all see depression and anxiety. We also see what we can call a reaction formation, in which we see a person who is overly good, who is constantly concerned with telling others how to behave and what is the right thing for them to do, and we begin to suspect that the holier than thou attitude may conceal considerable guilt in the individual over his own impulses.

Psychotherapeutically I always have to approach my own patients in terms of getting them to recognize the impulses for which they feel guilty and to make a very sharp distinction between their thoughts and what they actually have done. We will see this, for example, even in an individual who comes to us with a fear of homosexuality despite the fact that he has never had any homosexual activity; or we will see an individual with a fear of his own aggressiveness when he has never done anything which is outwardly aggressive. One particular area which we ordinarily don't touch upon is the guilt over the violation of ritualistic law. I see this occasionally in some of my very Orthodox patients where they become immensely concerned over the fact that they may have violated some of the ritualistic procedures with which they were brought up. We as psychiatrists will begin to delve further, and seek perhaps a sexual component or an aggressive component. In this area, statistics in the State of Massachusetts showed that the greatest percentage of schizophrenics in the Massachusetts State Hospital system were among the very Orthodox Catholics; in second place were the very Orthodox Jews (with the footnote that there were not enough of them to really say the statistics were quite valid). But we do find that where there is a high degree of Orthodoxy, the superego tends to be stronger, the guilt feeling tends to be stronger, and although I don't have any direct source of referral from the very Orthodox, I've seen any number of young men who have been Yeshiva *Buchas* having an enormous sense of guilt over their thoughts and over their feelings.

RABBI BOKSER : An important distinction has to be drawn between psychiatry and religion in order to avoid the suggestion that they are parallel disciplines. Psychiatry is a science, and a science expresses itself in a different language — in a language of exactness, of sober statement. It is meticulously careful not to overstate, to avoid the poetic turn of phrase, and to speak in an exact, precise fashion. Religion, because it isn't a science, because it is an attempt to moralize, expresses itself in a language that speaks to the imagination, to the heart, to the emotional side of man. It will therefore take on the limitations of literature and poetry. It will therefore exaggerate: it will overstate or understate.

There is no question that there is a distinction between feeling and deed, that it is easier to attain an innocence of deed than of feeling. But on the other hand I think we will all agree that there is a higher state reached by man, who even in his feeling has a state of innocence. Therefore, a person who speaks in the language of religion may exhort people to be virtuous even in their thoughts, even in their feelings. The Ten Commandments say: "Thou shalt not covet." Primarily this has to do with feelings. The psalmist tells us that to ascend the mountain of the Lord, a person must have clean hands and a pure heart. Of course, it's an exaggeration. Is there anybody who has clean hands and pure heart? Nobody really does. So in a certain sense you would say: "Nobody can go up to the mountain of the Lord." But when you understand it as literature you allow the psalmist the liberties of exaggerating. What he is really talking about is that a man should be watchful about his actions and about his thoughts.

In the confessional of the Day of Atonement we declare our remorse for the sins that we have committed with our eyes or with our thoughts. These phrases of a pathic nature that religion employs may, however, be taken literally; then we fashion a doctrine out of them and speculate whether it does or does not agree with Freud or some other school of psychology. Literalism may pose a problem for religion itself. If we take seriously, literally, this business of clean hands and a pure heart he may become burdened with a sense of guilt. A man knows that his heart isn't pure — it's full of many perversities; he will be troubled with an excessiveness of guilt.

Of course religion corrects itself by declaring — and I am

glad Dr. Gordis quoted it — "That there is no man so righteous that he is without sin." Tradition itself corrects itself by telling a man not to take his failings so seriously because there really isn't a man who is so righteous that he is without sin. Tradition doesn't define a righteous man as a man who is without sin, but as one in whom there is a preponderance of good deeds over evil deeds. This poses the question : how do you measure the preponderance? It isn't mathematical : one deed of Eichmann stands on the scale so heavy in the immensity of its crime that a million good deeds by somebody else will not compensate, will not balance it.

Religion in this sense makes an important contribution precisely because it does not talk primarily to the sick person; it talks to every man and it tells every man, "your life is shot through with limitations, with deficiencies, so that you have to struggle with yourself and you have to aim for the extreme, which is impossible of attainment — for clean hands and a pure heart." At the same time it cautions him not to exaggerate his sense of inadequacy. Incidentally in the literature, which calls for penitence, sometimes there is as much concern with assuring the man who feels guilty that there is therapy available to him. Its primary end is not in creating the feeling of guilt, as it is in making the man aware that he is a sinner and that he has to cleanse himself, that cleansing is open to him. Now, from the point of view of the moral stature of the man — which psychiatry doesn't come to grips with, but religion does : It challenges the man to feel his inadequacy, and to be aware that this is a permanent human condition and that it is true universally, but at the same time that this is the major burden of his life and that he must endlessly struggle to attain greater purity, cleanliness of hands.

One of the problems with which we must concern ourselves is not the guilt feeling but rather its absence. Sometimes I find that society conspires to desensitize the man so that instead of having guilt feelings this society will precisely rob him of this, which is one of his important assets as a man. The Nazis, for example, literally subjected their people to an elaborate treatment, which had as its major objective to desensitize the conscience or the superego, and to rob the German people of their guilt feelings. They did all kinds of things before a major action against Jews. In some instances they gave them liquor to drink, because when a man is drunk his superego is asleep; or they subjected them to conditioning movies and propaganda. Those that were to be guards in the concentration camps were subjected to brutalizing treatments. After certain exposures they became so used to seeing brutality that it no longer shocked them — and one of the problems that needs to be investigated is to see how even in democratic societies our culture sometimes creates certain subtle influencing pressures which inhibit the superego from functioning and which allow men to accept things that their conscience would not allow them to accept.

Another point which seems to be pertinent is this; In all other realms we know that there are variations of sensitivity, so that I can hear certain things that sound to me like music but somebody more sensitive will detect many false sounds and dismiss the performance as poor playing. There are sensitivities to music, there are sensitivities to painting. I went with my wife through a museum the other day, I saw one girl who was so enraptured by the picture she looked at that when I whispered something to my wife, this girl looked at me as though I had committed a frightful crime. Well, I understand it. Now it seems to me that we have to make allowances for the same kind of gradations in sensitivity, which in a very legitimate sense are present in the functioning of the superego. Also, that there are some people who have greater guilt feelings because of thoughts or deeds, because of what they did or what they didn't do, and we don't have to feel that a person who reacts more intensely than the norm is a queer. We have to allow the whole spectrum of variation, from the relatively minor to the so called norm through the exaggerated and extreme sensitivity, which enables one man to react to a harsh musical note as though something frightful has occurred, and that similarly expresses itself in a moral sense as something frightful, while somebody else passes by without feeling that there's anything wrong. The so called exaggerated or extreme responses to values or to guilt are not necessarily an indication of anything morbid or sick. Sometimes we would be more justified in calling them an expression of genius.

What is genius? Genius in music means that someone can express himself and react in a manner that the average man cannot reach. Perhaps we must also recognize a category of moral genius.

The final point that I want to make is this: You spoke at length about values as the conventions of society. Now I'm not saying that psychiatry necessarily would accept my point of view—this is something which has to do with philosophy—but I certainly wouldn't accept this definition of values. The greatest expression of value and the search for values has often been in defiance of society. Moses grew up in a society and in a home and in an atmosphere where slavery was quite normal —he rebelled against it. The Nazi society tried to indoctrinate its citizens along certain lines, but this did not legitimize this value system. As a matter of fact, whenever we find the emergence of new values in any society—and when we do we have the most dramatic moments in the moral history of mankind—we are dealing with individuals who defy society. I would say that such individuals represent for us the moral genius in action. These are people standing at the frontier of our moral order, not conditioned by their society or their family; but rather something else has happened: the miracle of creation all over again. Just as the symphonies of Beethoven didn't come from society and the paintings of Michaelangelo didn't come from society — but represented a new revelation — so I think in the realm of morals we are also dealing with many new revelations. We need to feel that perhaps we stand on holy ground when some of these geniuses deviate from the conventional thing to do to bear witness to a higher morality.

DR. ROBBINS : The psychiatrist recognizes apparent guilt and the presence of non-guilt. Does Judaism also recognize the utilization or pretense of guilt? That is, does it recognize the fact that an individual may not feel guilty and may really enjoy the fact that he is fooling his customers and short changing them as that butcher did; but when he feels depressed and the rabbi asks probing questions, or if he acts mean, let us say, in the synagogue, or doesn't give a contribution consonant with his means to Federation, will he invent a feeling of guilt to excuse himself? I think we certainly make a distinction between guilt as a rationalization on the part of which Dr. Nadell was talking about, for example, even on the part of the excessive moralists. There is also the excessive pseudo-guilt or the *mea culpa* attitude : "Well, I'm sorry, I shouldn't have done it," which tries, through that device, to absolve the person of any responsibility : "Go break a window and say I'm sorry." This doesn't repair the window and psychiatrists have to deal with that fact too. We might, as psychiatrists, ask ourselves, when a person commits a crime which everybody including the person who commits it agrees is a crime, such as the crime of incest, we might ask ourselves, as we do clinically, why did he do it? What were the factors in the disorganization of his personality that led to this act? Someone asked : "If a boy commits a crime — kills somebody because of certain things that happened to him at the hands of a cruel father and an unloving mother, and he developed such hate that in some later period of his life he should spill over and commit a crime because he was neurotically distorted by his upbringing, who is responsible? The murderer, and who else? Here is one distinction, perhaps. One may be able to explain through our science of personality why certain things happen. This neither explains nor condones. But there is a doubt, and it is a frequent accusation against psychiatry that it would give an explanation, and in doing so psychiatrists both accept and condone. They say, "The poor guy is sick," or make some such maudlin non-scientific statement.

Basically psychiatry derives from science and tries to define its terms rather than being poetic. It is intriguing, however, to know that Sigmund Freud was once considered for the Nobel Prize in Literature.

RABBI KAGAN: We are seriously concerned with what Judaism and Psychiatry have to say on this whole problem of rationalization as it applies to the most damaging guilt in Jewish history, namely the whole concept of the crucifixion; the accusation that we murdered God. If we accept the genius of Freud then we must consider his insights concerning the Oepidus conflicts. We know that the four-year-old boy has a fear of his father—perhaps it's his competition with his mother. At any rate, there is this four-year-old Christian boy who is taught that God the Father insisted that his son be killed to save mankind. Now a four-year-old Christian boy is not a theologian. His images are of a father and a son. If it is his father killing the son, and one way to rationalize away this guilt feeling (which is the primitive primordial guilt), is to say in the crucifixion story that it was not God's father who asked that his son be killed to save mankind, but the Jews who asked. This is a very serious twentieth-century psychological problem and only the Jews in general, and rabbis and Jewish psychiatrists can meet headlong this serious challenge to the future generations of American Jews as well as Jews throughout the world.

RABBI GORDIS : That is one form of psychosis of which Jews are entirely free. I never heard of a Jew who had guilt feelings for having killed "God."

RABBI KAGAN : I'm talking about the Christians.

RABBI GORDIS : We don't feel that we are guilty. Rather, it is they who say we are guilty. Therefore, it is essentially their problem and I doubt if we have any specific contribution to make in telling them how to handle the alleged murderer of their God.

RABBI KAGAN : There are effective methods that Christians have to use. There are Jewish experts in the field of psychology and psychiatry who have much to say to the Christian world as to what our respective educational methods should be in dealing with this problem.

RABBI SANDROW : We ought to focus our attention primarily on how these two disciplines can enrich the individual and specifically the individual Jew. Some of us have been very much concerned about the need for an understanding of the psychiatric discipline in various theological seminaries. This is a kind of group therapy too; I think that I could have been a better rabbi, if in the earlier days, the days of my studies at the Seminary, there had been a course in which I could have understood how to deal with people and to recognize that deviant behavior, emotional behavior. It is my hope that whatever comes out of our discussions will also have some bearing on what various theological seminaries, Orthodox, Reform, Conservative, are trying to do with rabbinical students. Wherever one goes nowadays one meets a rabbi who is an amateur "psychiatrist." This is a dangerous thing. These are separate disciplines: religion has a point of view, and an attitude towards morality; psychiatry also has an approach to these matters. Dr. Gordis said that psychiatrists are neutral. But they are not quite so neutral as the people on the outside world imagine them to be.

The psychiatrist has a glorious opportunity to do something with a normally moderately sick person. When he shields this person, when he treats this person — and I may be wrong, and it may be contrary to the science of psychiatry — he can do something about indicating a kind of a judgment with regard to specific acts. This is an area to which we can address ourselves. The rabbis are expected to be authoritative. The psychiatrist expects a rabbi to be as authoritative as Rabbi Gordis was with his butcher. Psychiatrists cannot be authoritative. Some of the outstanding members of my congregation have been psychoanalyzed. During this process I think it would have helped them a great deal to feel that when they were released from their treatment the psychiatrist had somehow or other said to them, "This is right," and "This is wrong," and "This is the way I feel about it." By doing this we could go a long way toward dispelling the notion that the psychiatrist is non-judgmental. Sometimes in being non-judgmental he is judgmental.

How does the religious practitioner recognize that the individual is in the state of mind or emotion which requires psychiatric treatment? This is an important matter to which we have to address ourselves. There are many simple problems that people have which we as rabbis can handle without sending them to a psychiatrist. Do we merely indicate that the religious law says A, B, C, D, "this you shall do, this you shall not do?" How do you take up this religious, authoritative, legal and moral area with the individual after he has been released from treatment?

DR. MONTAGU ULLMAN: Rabbi Gordis's reference to the amorality of the psychiatric situation is really a common myth. Amorality means "without morals." Now, a psychiatrist is a psychiatrist by virtue of his understanding and application of problems of morality. Actually, as in every communication to a patient at a verbal or a non-verbal level, he is indicating what he likes, what he prefers, what he wants, what he expects, and what he is striving for. He is always making a judgment when he selects from what the patient brings to him as to what is important and what is not, what is healthy and what is not. These are basically related to his own moral fiber, his ability to translate morality into a clinical situation. There is a difference in approach to the question of morality that intrigues the theologian: that the psychiatrist does identify that this act is right and this act is wrong, but his concern is primarily with the capacity of the individual to deal with the rightness or the wrongness of the act. The act has to be identified as right or wrong, but this is not his major concern as it is in the case of the law or in other situations. He has to concern himself with the question of the ability of the individual and how that ability can be engendered, nurtured, developed, and in some instances created; so that he is concerned with the question of guilt in a different sense and in a process sense. He is concerned with the information he can get about the context of the act he has identified. He has to get at the context, just as putting a knife in a person's abdomen in one context is a sadistic, aggressive, destructive act, but in an operating room, in the hands of a surgeon it is a constructive, health-giving act. It may be a very similar actual action. Psychiatry, like the Jewish religion, is not monolithic and there are differences of point of view. I find myself congenially drawn to the notion that man is born straight and that somehow he is pushed or falls off that straight path. I come from the so-called culturalist swing of things in the psychiatric spectrum and find this approach more congenial to my own thinking, so that I'm more concerned with what it has been than with the fall from the potential grace. Man's only inheritance is for potential grace, for potential health, and unfortunately men as social beings have never solved the problem of how to live together to the point that they can evoke from each other the full measure of their human potential. Concerning the term "guilt," we must realize that we are using it in many different contexts. We are talking about guilt in a religious sense, in a realistic sense, and in a legal sense. We are talking about neurotic guilt, and we ought to define more of the nature of neurotic guilt. It is not guilt at all, and it has a lot to do, perhaps, with rationalization—a kind of neurotic maneuvering in the world. It lacks the quality of real guilt: it lacks the capacity for remorse; genuine guilt is associated with remorse—with the kind of insight that can make the person less guilty or not guilty at all the next time he is in that situation. Neurotic guilt is anxiety; is a closed circuit; is someone who is forced into a compulsive kind of activity which he cannot evaluate but is forced to do for protection from anxiety. This is his atonement—his way of paying off in relation to something he has to do and has no control over if the lack of control has the key quality for the psychiatrist.

RABBI KAGAN: We try to make the distinction between existation guilt, which is a religious subject, and pathological guilt which we deal with.

DR. FRANZBLAU: First, with regard to Rabbi Sandrow's implicit feeling about psychiatry that a psychiatrist is non-judgmental and should be judgmental, surely he doesn't mean by this that the psychiatrist must be punitive, that he must take a stand in favor of a particular code of ethics or morals. To be non-judgmental, in the mind of the psychiatrist concerning the individual who stands before him, the psychiatrist receives him with the desire to hold up a mirror to this man's inner feelings, to reveal what is going on in the depths of his unconscious and not to make judgments of a moral nature which might prevent the man from reaching the root of his difficulty and thereby remedying it. Second, in the question of engendering guilt, the psychiatrist does not always relieve guilt. Very often the psychiatrist and the analyst helps the individual who does not see wherein he has offended—against his own self, or against his dear ones, or against the society to recognize wherein the guilt lies, and then to take the necessary steps toward regeneration. Merely to have insight, which many laymen feel is the great washing corrector of all wrong in man, is not sufficient even in the therapeutic process. Rather, it is necessary in the therapeutic process to have the perception that the individual has with reference to his own error and his own behavior become such a part of future conflict and future behavior that every muscle, every fibre, every thought that the individual has thereafter conforms to new resources and new moral insights. It would be wrong to say that the psychiatrist is not interested in morality. Quite the contrary. The psychiatrist goes to the very root of human morality when he gets interested in the development of the conscience that is either overly strong or too weak. Gustave Eichorn was one of Freud's disciples and did the basic work with regard to the treatment of criminality and delinquency in youngsters. He pointed out that you have to first make the individual neurotic, in other words you have to instill first of all a sense of the code of society before you can proceed to cure his neurotic guilt.

It is so easy to talk about religion as though we meant one particular thing. But religion, of course, is a very varied thing. Religion is a dome of many-colored glass and sometimes it's almost opaque in the density that it presents to mankind—and in the inability of man to exist under it except with neurotic conflict and neurotic result. Nietzsche said that "Christianity put a drop of poison in the cup of Eros," and if you compare and contrast the Jewish attitude on the subject of sin with the Christian attitude towards sex, you concede that the God itself in Christianity is a completely asexual God. The virgin mother, the virgin birth, the absence of fatherhood — sexless except in the intervention of the Holy Ghost which is the only sexually potent entity in the Godhead.

The attitude of Christianity toward the whole question of sex and sexuality necessarily must influence, color, and shape the attitude of the Christian to his daily life. In Judaism fortunately we do not have any such conception. Perhaps there may be a reason why the vast majority of psychoanalysts and psychiatrists, Freud himself and the vast percentage of his disciples, are Jews. It is a much more comfortable milieu for a Jew to operate in than it is for a Catholic. That is perhaps why there are so few Catholic psychiatrists and psychoanalysts. The prevalence of psychiatry in Catholic Europe for example is negligible. In reality the opposition of the Papacy to psychoanalysis has just recently within the last decade or so been effectively broken in spite of the original encyclical of Pope Pius XII, so that we have to define our terms in our work in Judaism and as Jewish psychiatrists.

In psychiatry we have an entirely different problem. If the Jewish religious bodies could somehow help further to release what could be called ecclesialgenic guilt — to release the guilt which an individual within Judaism has, not from violation of ethical codes or ethical behavior, but from the violation of ritual codes and ritual behavior, we could make a significant contribution in this area.

JUDGE LEVY : I want to make clear that a judge is not a layman in this field and cannot be relegated to a position of mere observation in matters concerned with the criminally insane defendant. When it is the judge's misfortune, as well as his responsibility to preside at a court such as the Bellevue General Court, it is important to understand that it is the judge—after receiving the professional advice of the psychiatrist, the views of the rabbi, the assistance of the social worker—who under our system of laws has the ultimate determination to make. It is the judge who in our judicial process must distinguish between the person who is mentally or emotionally ill, who is mentally disturbed, who is mentally or emotionally hazardous to himself or to others, or who is viciously or criminally insane. We must protect all of those who appear before us in the light of due process, whatever the rabbi may think, indeed whatever the psychiatrist thinks. We would like you to agree among yourselves so that when we do have that serious ultimate responsibility of determination we can feel that religious moral precepts and science and literature, if you will, of psychiatry will be of fundamental assistance in the determination and the definition of what we have to do.

DR. RADEMAN: I'm only concerned with one sentence —perhaps I didn't hear it correctly—a sentence of Dr. Franzblau's which I think will be an area very much worthy of exploration in the future, but I think reveals immediately one attitude that is always judgmental—dangerously judgmental, as a matter of fact—I'm a little surprised because it hasn't happened yet in all of my experience as a psychiatrist, and I've had that problem, because Dr. Franzblau assumed in his statement that there was, or there had to be, a difference between two types of conducts. One type of conduct which immediately places higher in a hierarchy of values, the multi-moraled, that is, moral conduct and that which we simply regard as ritualistic.

But I feel that in all fairness to those who have strong religious commitment to a total religious tradition, the psychiatrist must remain — as I believe he is — most fair. In most cases that I have experience with he does no more than what he is expected, which is to use the mirror; to use the mirror for the sighting of the orthodox or ritualistically committed individuals. Now to find out whether his guilt with regard to the desecration of the Sabbath or eating of non-kosher food, or co-habiting with a niece — which might be legal with us, moral non-incestuous with Jews but incestuous for Christians — to do no more than to put up a psyche to see whether this behavior is neurotic — neurotically, shall I say — caused, oriented, and no more than that; because the minute the psychiatrist starts, in his own mind, thinking that this is unimportant, he places in jeopardy the type of creative religiosity within the situation of the type of situation that Rabbi Bokser described.

RABBI EDWARD KLEIN: It is my purpose in this treatise to speak frankly of an occasional interdisciplinary conflict and an indication for an interdisciplinary approach, to the problems of our people. Experience and at least one recent survey indicate that the majority of people with problems consult their clergyman first. This is certainly true of Judaism, for the Rabbi has served traditionally as teacher and judge, not merely in ritual matters but also in interpersonal relationships and moral problems. Even in our sophisticated age, when tradition as a whole is a motivating factor, people in trouble tend to turn to the rabbi first, because rightly or wrongly they view their problem in moral terms and resist the still prevalent stigma of needing a psychiatrist. Thus, if there is a marital problem — even though the problem may stem from some deep-rooted emotional conflict — the person is likely to seek out the rabbi who solemnized the marriage, and if there is a parent–child conflict even though there may be strong indications of personality disorder the rabbi as teacher and arbiter is frequently the first to be sought out. The rabbi who has some training and experience in psychology will know to what extent his counsel can be effective and where further ministrations by him may prove harmful. It is at this point that he must make a referral to a competent psychiatrist, and it is precisely here that he encounters difficulty.

The client may demur, still feeling that the problem needs only surface treatment. Sometimes he raises objections to what he believes to be the standard psychiatric procedures of a three-year depth analysis and to the high cost involved. The patient clergyman may overcome the first hurdle by explaining the eclectic approach of many psychiatrists and disabusing the client of some popular misconceptions, but he is all too frequently stymied by the next hurdle. Where can he find a psychiatrist whose fees the client can afford, or where can he find a clinic or social agency to serve him promptly without the usual long wait?

Let us assume that all hurdles are overcome: the rabbi refers a client to a private or agency psychiatrist. All too frequently the contact between rabbi and therapist ends there. The rabbi who has assumed the initial responsibility wishes to know something of the person's progress. A call to the psychiatrist often results in a non-committal, non-communicative answer. This is particularly frustrating when the client continues to have contact with the rabbi as a member of the congregation or participant in its activities. If it is a young person, should he be encouraged to attend the youth dances; should a special effort be made to involve him in committee work; can or should he assume responsibility at this juncture? The psychiatrist, hesitating to convey privileged information to the rabbi, sometimes keeps him in the dark.

There is an additional problem when the rabbi is contacted by anxious members of the client's family. How is the client doing? The rabbi isn't sure because he really doesn't know. Psychiatrists for obvious reasons sometimes keep the client's family at arm's length. An understanding rabbi with even a modicum of information from the psychiatrist might allay the family's anxieties and even help the client indirectly by helping to contribute to the peace of the household. A recent experience illustrates this point:

Parents expressed grave concern about a twenty-year-old girl under analysis for two years who suddenly moved out of the house. There has been no communication between parents and daughter. Inquiries of the therapist revealed only the suggestion, "leave your daughter alone." Inquiry by the rabbi proved similarly fruitless, nor could a second psychiatrist known to the rabbi evoke a response from the therapist. To the parents' query, "Are we to give our daughter up?" the rabbi could give no answer.

This is not meant to be a reflection—even by indirection—on the vital role of the psychiatrist and psychiatry. Nor is there a reluctance to admit that rabbis too are often to blame. Sometimes the rabbi tries to be a psychiatrist. Often he lacks the understanding to interpret the psychiatrist's role. This discussion is meant, however, to plead for more complete understanding between rabbi and psychiatrist, for fuller communication between the two. The psychiatrist's role is indisputable, but so is the rabbi's. Analysis is a recognized therapeutic technique, but since this is equally as important to the client's care, sooner or later he must be related to his fellows in meaningful activities—must fashion a philosophy that holds life to be worth living and find goals that are worth living for. Here the services of the rabbi are indicated and the activities of the congregation also; for it serves not only as a house of prayer where the soul's windows are open to the light of God's love, but also is a house of study where the Jewish way of life is taught, and a house of assembly where people are related to each other in an atmosphere of sociability and fellowship.

DR. WORTIS : There are two lines of discussion : One to discuss questions of theory, approach, ideology, etc. and one to discuss practical problems of inter-relationships between psychiatrists and rabbis. I avoid the deep waters of ideological discussion because it is much easier to talk of the practical things first and to allow a lot of time and opportunity to thrash out these more complex questions of theory and approach.

If we want to discuss the problem of how rabbis, in the course of their work, should deal with problems of psychiatric disorder, and how and when they should confer with or refer to psychiatrists, it would be helpful to define our terms and to get a picture of the scope of the problem, which will affect our style of approach. The recent study of a typical adult population, called *Mental Health in the Metropolis,* by workers headed by Dr. Stroll, found that roughly $\frac{1}{4}$ of this adult population was more or less seriously bothered by psychiatric complaints. The exact figure is 23.4 per cent. And another quarter of the population; if you like exact figures 21.8 per cent; had moderately-severe psychiatric symptoms. In another approximate third of the adult population; aged twenty to fifty-nine; 36.3 per cent had mild symptoms and less than one/fifth of the adult population, 18.5 per cent, were regarded by the examining professional people, as symptom-free. I have often distributed paper, and asked people to put a little plus mark on the paper if they regarded themselves more or less neurotic, and a minus mark if they thought they weren't. I did it recently with a group of medical students. I can safely predict that if the number of pluses that come back were unusually low, they would be in the 65 per cent range and if they were as I rather expect they would be, they would be in the 80–90 per cent range. With my medical students it was 90 per cent. There was only one x in a group of ten that put a minus mark down.

Now these, of course, are self-diagnoses. But it is the self-diagnoses of people that drives them to seek help so that it is a significant statistic. A small percentage—half of one per cent— of this adult population were sufficiently disturbed to be institutionalized. We can forget them; they amount to a small percentage for our purposes.

This is only the general population; what about the Jewish population? Well, this book has a breakdown on religious groups too, and for what satisfaction it may be worth to us we find that in the Jewish adult population, there was a slight tendency to have fewer of the most seriously disturbed, but also a tendency to show fewer of the entirely well, so that there is a tendency to cluster toward the middle—the milder moderately disturbed. And the differences amount to only a few per cent, so I think that for practical purposes we have to concede that at least a half or more of our adult population shows enough psychiatric symptoms to make it a matter of concern to them, if not to others, and perhaps a higher percentage, if they're sophisticated, well-educated etc., might even exaggerate the degree to which they need help.

Thus the problem of when should the rabbi call the psychiatrist in is a serious one. In fact, where does the rabbi start giving his time to people who think they are in need of help and who are in trouble? It means that out of every seven adult Jews in New York City, only one can be said to be free of psychiatric symptoms. These are tension, worry, sleeplessness, excessive drinking, seriously excessive smoking, a whole list of common complaints listed in this study. It is perfectly obvious that there are not enough, will never be enough; and I would add, in my opinion, should never be enough psychiatrists to give treatment to everybody with psychiatric symptoms or complaints. They have to be discriminating and how do you discriminate?

People differ in their judgment about how one discriminates.

Now I'm sure if we conducted a little canvass among the rabbis we'd find at one end of the spectrum some trigger-happy rabbis who are able to call in psychiatrists when any member of his congregation says "boo," and at the other end of the spectrum rabbis who never refer a member of their congregation to psychiatrists. So there is no uniformity that exists, nor can we expect any. Of course, there are many rabbis who prefer to give spiritual guidance themselves, but even there they have to be discriminating, if they're not going to be overwhelmed either by large numbers or by persistent members of their congregation who feel they have to see them twice a week and call them up every second evening. How do you discriminate? Well you might ask the psychiatrists how they discriminate. But unfortunately I must say you'll find almost as much variety of judgment among the psychiatrists as you find among the rabbis. Let us face the facts: psychiatrists are not in agreement with each other; they differ about a number of important matters and if rabbis are to talk of a cooperative relationship with psychiatrists as adults and as people of education and understanding, I think it would be of no use to evade a realistic appraisal of the psychiatric situation because in the final analysis, as I will emphasize, the rabbi will have to make some judgments.

What do psychiatrists disagree about? They disagree about the point when ordinary troubles, worries, and tensions become a disease or disorder that needs treatment. They have different points of view about this: some psychiatrists are very strict, rather narrow in their concept of what constitutes a *bona fide* psychiatric disorder or disease, and some of my colleagues would have no hesitation in saying half the population either need or could benefit from some form of psychiatric treatment and some would go further than that. These are, I think, honest statements of differences of point of view among us.

We psychiatrists also disagree about the causes of these

psychiatric symptoms. Some psychiatrists think almost all psychiatric symptoms are caused by more-or-less internal subjective conflicts related to unconscious factors, with a heavy importance laid on early family life, forgotten experiences, and other things. Other psychiatrists are more inclined to emphasize the importance of adult experience, the situation in which a person finds himself or has been living in recent years. And even those psychiatrists who think of the importance of daily experience and the vicissitudes of life differ in the emphasis they would place on an individual's immediate experience: i.e.—how he relates to his wife, his children, his place of employment. Some have more sweep to their concept of environment and will emphasize the importance of the culture of the social group a person belongs to. Obviously this affects their style of approach towards the case. Perhaps it also tends to emphasize the importance of larger group cultural experiences. Such psychiatrists will take a more modest view of what they can hope to accomplish in a one-to-one relationship with a patient.

Those who confine their interests to, what they think is important, the narrow framework of an individual's personal experiences will feel a bit more confident about what they can do to change this individual's life experiences. So that theory also affects practice. Then too, there are those psychiatrists who hardly give any thought to the physical health of their patients. It is true that a person may have been heavily addicted to alcohol for years, may have all kinds of ailments, may suffer from insomnia and infections, and may be in so weakened a state that he doesn't have the energy to do what he knows he ought to do; and there are psychiatrists who allow these considerations to enter into their analysis of the problem of their treatment of the case. But there are other psychiatrists who are unaccustomed, by habit and theory, to consider physical factors such as physical makeup, age of the patient, presence or absence of menopausal changes with change of life, and there are important ranges of difference in the emphasis psychiatrists accord to these things and the attention they give them in their treatment.

Finally there are some psychiatrists, among whom I count myself, who are very conscious of their ignorance of some of the things which cause these disorders, and being conscious of our ignorance we are not very glib or certain in our answers, or perhaps, we are more cautious in our approach. I have other colleagues, whom in a sense I can only envy, who have facile answers for all of the problems that they encounter; so you encounter ranges of the confidence, knowledge, and insight among psychiatrists. Now with these differences in approach obviously you will find differences in treatment, in attitudes, and in concept of where the psychiatrist fits in.

Obviously, if the psychiatrist is convinced that subjective, internal, unconscious conflicts are the primary factors in most psychiatric disorders, he will feel quite sure that the way to deal with them is primarily in the prolonged one-to-one relationship with the patient where he can bring these unconscious conflicts to the surface and by a process of internal rearrangement effect a cure. But if the psychiatrist in general or in particular in a certain case is convinced that this person's job is getting him down, and that he is just in an impossible situation he will perhaps attach more importance to giving some explicit advice — or, if the advice can't readily be given or couldn't be acted upon when given, he might settle for half and say "there are limits to what I can do with psychiatric treatment; there are factors in this case that are just not easily amenable to change." So you have differences among psychiatrists in what might be termed their passivity or activity in terms of trying to influence the patient's life or giving advice.

Of course, there are also psychiatrists who will never prescribe a sedative because they believe the mental processes are always primary, and those who use judicious medication from time to time and even will apply types of treatment that involve a physical component. Further, at one extreme there are people I wouldn't call them psychiatrists but people who practice psychiatry, who are completely opposed to any psychological interest. They either say: "too bad, a person is born this way; it's in his blood; it's just his constitutional makeup," and they will either profess a nihilistic attitude or glibly prescribe some pills and let it go at that. We have such practitioners, unfortunately.

What does a rabbi do in the face of this situation? A mere general reference to the need for rabbis to use psychiatrists more will satisfy the practical situation as rabbis find it. I think the rabbi cannot escape the obligation to engage in some discussion on these matters, and to acquire, if not some convictions, at least some predilections, to have some people whose ability and whose good judgment they can respect, and not to speak in too breezy, offhand or general way about psychiatry or the need of psychiatry. In other words some intelligence and more-or-less informed discrimination has to be exercised by the rabbi if he enters into this area altogether — which means discussion groups, reading, study, perhaps this study could well begin in the theological seminary where it would at least hasten the process of some orientation in an area which is bewildering even to the experts.

As for referral, it would be easier to start with the more obvious cases and then get down to the more controversial material. Certainly a patient or a member of a congregation who is obviously psychotic, who has broken down, who cannot think straight, who has delusions and hallucinations, or exhibits other earmarks of quite serious derangement, should absolutely be referred to a good psychiatrist — a psychiatrist whose good judgment and clinical experience the rabbi can learn to respect.

It would not be difficult to teach a rabbi if he does not already know what the earmarks of some of the common psychoses are. Profound immobilization, what in psychiatry we call depressions; where all of the functions are depleted; where the person is like a run-down battery and doesn't have the energy to think, to move, to master the everyday problems of life; where every problem overwhelms him and he thinks of no way out, except perhaps through suicide, these depressions are by no means uncommon and must be kept distinct in one's thinking from the ordinary worries and cares of everyday life, and a depression, once it is recognized or even suspected should be referred to a psychiatrist. Evidences of disordered thinking or disorganization of thought require referral to a psychiatrist. Wild excitements, outlandish excitements, what we call manic states, where people start telegraphing the President, sending fire alarms and such—these certainly are not the type of case that a rabbi should closet himself with and seek to persuade the person that he should be referred to the psychiatrist. Where there are obvious important medical components to a problem, it would be safe to refer a member of the congregation to a psychiatrist: where there is drug addiction involved, severe insomnia, alcoholism, or where there are other outcroppings associated with symptoms in the physical realm, such as ulcers and whatnot, certainly it would be wise to have the medically trained psychiatrist in on the case. Indeed, this is necessary wherever a neurotic conflict or neurotic anxiety or habits of thought or behavior seem particularly perplexing and present a very severe symptomatology and very forbidding symptoms which you feel you cannot begin to comprehend. At this level of complexity it would be a good safeguard to see that you have at least the benefit of a psychiatric opinion before you got beyond your depth.

Finally, in all these cases where there are actual dangers

involved—homicidal dangers, suicidal dangers, dangers of physical assault—it would be better and wiser not to tamper with any of them. These then are the more obvious reasons why certain people who come to a rabbi for help should be referred to a medical practitioner. I say "medical practitioner" though I well know that there are practitioners in this field who are not physicians, because, as you will see, almost by definition a problem which is sufficiently serious to need a physician who is a psychiatrist. Problems which are more psychiatric are generally sufficiently serious to need a physician who is a psychiatrist. In problems which are more or less purely psychological, not only is the physician not necessary but he is often undesirable; there are too many such problems around. But here too, I'm not so sure I would use the word "treatment" in dealing with them. These milder disorders, which arise in everyday life in so many people, are so common and so numerous, that as a matter of good public health judgment and planning we have to concede that many different agencies, both of a non-professional as well as a professional nature, must be implicated in dealing with this mammoth public health problem. With children the teachers are important, with guidance counselors, with adults, certainly rabbis are important, and also friends and relatives so far as they can exercise good judgment. Actually most of our confusions will involve this group of milder problems: the anxieties, the tensions, the worries, the habits, the character, the malformations and so on of everyday life, that one doesn't quite know where psychiatry leaves off and where common sense or the mediation of other interested and sympathetic people begins.

Hereafter the rabbi will have to learn to exercise some judgment of his own. We don't call the surgeon in when our child gets a splinter, and we don't hesitate to give members of our family advice with their personal problems. The transition is a gradual one from this homely type of mutual help to what we can say with a long and serious face constitutes psycho-therapy or psychiatric treatment. I can see no clear line of demarcation and would both concede and urge that we think of the whole spectrum of influences on people and their every-day problems, which can be wholesome and helpful. I would urge that the rabbi who deals with these problems as part of his everyday interests and responsibility have easy access to a psychiatrist who will teach him, assist him, and to some degree train him and always help him to deal with these problems without making serious missteps.

One of the things we can hope to accomplish is to develop a working relationship so that the overload on psychiatrists can be shared in part at least by the informed, the interested, the sympathetic, and even the scientifically minded rabbi who knows how to be helpful without making too much of a small problem or too little of a big one. A certain amount of helpful cooperative effort can be planned for, and can be achieved if we put our mind to it. This form may take the help of some occasional workshops, discussion groups, or occasional diagnos-tic consultations just to reassure the rabbi that he hasn't missed something important, or perhaps even the sharing in the management of problems where a psychiatrist will see a case occasionally, or where over a period of time a rabbi can carry the bulk of the responsibility.

Here too we confront questions of theory and if one belongs to a certain school of thought in psychiatry, one is over-respectful of the need for privacy, secrecy, and exclusiveness in the relationship, it is not likely that the person adhering to that point of view would want to share the responsibility for management with a rabbi, or with a teacher, or with others who may be involved. But, most psychiatrists today, you might say, under the sheer necessity of the demands for their help are growing more and more willing to share these responsibilities. In the case that Rabbi Klein mentioned of the psychiatrist who refused to share any information about the case, or to join forces with the rabbi in helping the case, it may be that the psychiatrist used sound judgment, but it also may be that he was too exclusive in his point of view. I have long ago learned that it is no breach of professional confidence to tell a patient who is in your office, "look here, you need help from sources (in your family or from your rabbi) besides me. How would it be if I told the rabbi this and that." You must then let the patient know exactly what you are going to tell the rabbi so that he doesn't have the feeling you are engaging in a colloquy behind his back.

With this assent and understanding of the patient it is often possible to introduce the helpful intercession of parents, even of friends, or of interested professional people like a rabbi to assist in the process. This is a question of the psychiatrist's style of work.

Then there is the question of money and it is a distressingly important question, because I would say that everywhere in the area of medical services we have chaotic conditions prevailing.

Psychiatry is, if anything, somewhat more chaotic than the other areas of medical services, largely because of the inordinate demands the present atmosphere has created for psychiatric services. In the privacy of our meetings we psychiatrists would concede that psychiatry has been overplayed in this country. People expect too much and expect intercession from us too often. So we have to retreat to more reasonable provinces of responsibility if we are to be useful. Somewhere down the line we have to concede that not only are psychiatrists called to help much too often but in those instances where they could be helpful the costs are frequently prohibitive. Rabbis, if they get involved in this problem — as they're bound to — should share the interests that most of us have in a promotion of more rational planning and more equitable distribution of psychiatric services through some such rational plan in the not-too-distant future.

Whether it is through the health insurance agencies or whether it is through some great scheme that Federation may work out some day, I do not know, but solutions must be found and in the meantime we will do what we can in the way of compromises. It is a serious problem and a meaningful problem. I also belong to that group of psychiatrists who not only disagree with the view that a patient must pay for his services for them to be helpful, but I think patients by and large would particularly benefit from their services if they didn't have to pay. It is bad enough to be sick without being taxed by an additional burden of expenses to carry at the time when you are least able to do so. This is an area that needs thoughtful consideration.

In conclusion, if we face up to the realities of the life problems of the people we deal with, we are forced to the realization that it takes more than the best of psychiatrists to cure most of the troubles and the tensions that the people encounter in everyday life, which means we have to set both modest and realistic goals in our dealings with these everyday problems. This is not to imply that there are not patients who can be brought back to wholesomeness and healthiness if we are skillful enough and if their disability is of that sort. But for everyone for whom we can produce complete recovery, there are many more in whom we will have to be satisfied with amelioration, with help, and with compromises until the larger circumstances in which this patient's problem develops are relieved by conditions which are an improvement over what they have to face daily.

Dr. Kagan : In Mount Vernon, New York, a psychiatrist has been handling what you might call a pathological delinquent — an adopted son, in a family where there are two adopted children. In this case the family was recommended by their rabbi to come to see me. I saw this lad about five times and gave him a Rorschach and a few other tests. I knew from the results that I would be involved beyond my depth and recommended psychiatric treatment. I then discovered from the family that he had been in psychiatric treatment since the age of six, and had already been through three psychiatrists. We felt that this young boy was ready for institutional treatment. He is now at such an institution. But my job as the rabbi in this situation, even though the family recognized me as a psychologist, with a license to practice psychology in the State of New York, was to function as a rabbi with, of course, a psychological orientation. My role was to orient the father and mother to accept this situation. All the while this lad was in the hands of the psychiatrist, who knew he couldn't do a damn thing for him, who had the boy for about twenty-five hours of consultation. During all those twenty-five hours, he had constantly reiterated to me: "Rabbi, *tzivill Gornisht Helfin.*" So my job with this family was to prepare them to accept this situation. This fortunately I was able to do and to counsel the father and the mother singly and together, and as a result the boy is now in Devereaux.

I am distressed by the fact that there are some of Dr. Wortis's colleagues who apparently don't belong to his school, who still feel that when there is a serious emotional problem, while the patient is undergoing treatment one must not, under any circumstances, reveal the situation to anyone. As Rabbi Klein pointed out, these psychiatrists will not reveal the situation to the members of the family or to the rabbi but let's speak about the members of the family: I can't understand it sometimes, and perhaps I don't know enough about it, perhaps the man is right in his judgment, but I often think to myself, if a patient suffers from some organic ailment, some very serious disease, from a cancer, say, would he not say, "I want to discuss the

situation with the members of your family because I think
you're not well." But when I want to talk to the members of
the family why is it that when it comes to the realm of the
mind, the realm of the emotions — that does not apply. You
cannot say to the patient, "I want to discuss this with the
members of your family because I think you're seriously ill,
you require a, b, c, and d."

There was such a situation, a very serious situation: this
person had been under treatment on a number of occasions;
he had symptoms of depression, has gone through series of
amelioration, as it were, and I have a feeling that if the
psychiatrists once and for all said, "look this is not going to
be good, I've got to take this up with the family, you're
shirking, you're going from one psychiatrist to another." In this
particular case this man's been to three psychiatrists already,
I do think that something has to be done in this area. I think
that the psychiatrist has a responsibility as a medical practitioner to tell the patient, "I would like to discuss this with
the members of your family."

I agree with you by and large, but please keep in mind two
considerations, both of which I mentioned; one is the legality
of the situation; the relationship to a doctor is a confidential
relationship, by law you cannot reveal information without the
consent of the patient you treated. If a twenty-year-old girl
comes to me on Monday and I hear a voice on the phone on
Tuesday asking if her daughter came to see me, I do not have
the right to tell this person that, because it's breach of a
confidential relationship. The second consideration is the question of tactics. You have to exercise judgment in your tactics
and you cannot always tactfully or tactically share a problem
if the timing is not right and the attitude of the patient is not
right and if the person to whom you turn is not right.

DR. ROBBINS: I certainly agree that there is a tendency of

many psychiatrists to overdo the matter of communication to responsible members of the family and in this connection I think we should discuss the rabbi as a quasi-member of the family. I mean he is the intermediary between the family and the patient in some of these situations. I shall leave out ridiculous excesses where there's a point of view that is extreme, or for certain individuals for whom there is never an exception. But we have to recognize two factors; one Dr. Franzblau referred to before, when he was referring to the difference between the non-moral not amoral position that we take in order to elicit the fullest communication from the patient as we hold the mirror up to him. If the patient feels in any way that what he shares with us in confidence and in privacy is going to be communicated to others, this blots his communication and interferes with the treatment, destroys the therapeutic relationship which transcends — let's say the anxiety of the parents or other responsible people. We're not talking about those patients who are not competent to make judgments themselves; if a person is psychotic you have to sometimes take that into consideration, and we're not talking about that extreme instance where somebody is going out and kills himself or does something self-destructive. Such a person is not personally responsible. We're assuming a reasonable degree of self responsibility in the patient.

The second factor is (and I'll show you a bridge in a moment), that psychiatric illnesses are manifested largely in interpersonal relationships. The manifest symptoms are usually or frequently interpersonal, that is, not merely that the patient is anxious, depressed, or has a mood disturbance but is often manifested in the life patterns of the person and impinge in one way or another on the immediate members of his family. They may be impinging on him, he may be impinging on them, they're usually impinging on each other. This is quite different than if a man has an ingrown toenail. The inquiry of the relative is often not merely an inquiry of interest, but an inquiry of guilt, an inquiry of coercion, an inquiry of nuisance in the treatment process; and you have to make a differential diagnosis as to what is the basis for the inquiry, why do they need to know. There may be legitimate reasons, but the circumstances of why they need to know may not be necessarily in the interest of the patient. Suppose, for example, the patient is a married man who has gonorrhea. You then have a physical illness with an interpersonal problem. Can you tell his wife — she has a right to know why he has pains at night and she has concern about her husband — can you say "Mrs. Jones he's all right, he just has a bad case of gonorrhea." I agree with Dr. Wortis one hundred per cent. I have frequently been in situations where a person has a right to inquire. I don't think the rabbi always has a right to inquire; he may have a legitimate reason to inquire, but not necessarily a right. Even then you have to make judgments which are not always easy.